Praise for *The Pug List*

This is a beautiful story, and beautifully told, of family and loss and love and rebuilding. Alison Hodgson's love for literature is evident on every page.

Shauna Niequist, author of *Bread & Wine* and *Savor.*

You don't have to like pugs to love this book. You'll laugh and cry as you follow the family's adventures through tragedy and triumphs, facing it all with honesty, faith, and humor.

Dale Hanson Bourke, author

At long last, research is confirming what dog lovers already know: Each dog is a unique, sentient being with a complex personality. And Oliver, the snorty little black dog of *The Pug List*, has more personality, and less bladder control, than most. I'm in love with this powerful story about a hurting family who adopts and is adopted by an unforgettable dog that makes a little girl named Eden smile once again.

Susy Flory, *New York Times* bestselling author or coauthor of ten books, including *Thunder Dog* and *Painting with Metro.*

A beautifully penned story of resilience and recovery, *The Pug List* is an inspirational memoir for anyone who has ever loved and lost. This family's emotional journey provides a poignant lesson from a hopeful little girl and a troublesome pug to remind us that love is always worth the struggle.

Julie Cantrell, *New York Times* and *USA Today* bestselling author of *The Feathered Bone*

I loved this story—heart-wrenching, heartwarming, and ultimately life-affirming. Alison Hodgson shows us very clearly the wonderful impact a dog can have on a family and the spiritual truth they teach us. Highly recommended.

Jim Kraus, author of *The Dog That Saved Stewart Coolidge* and *The Dog That Whispered*

By turns sweet and terrifying, Alison Hodgson takes us on a journey through the rebuilding of a house and a home. Regaining trust, recovering personalities, and adding a fur kid to the family on the way, she talks without sentimentality about the love of God for us, the love of mothers for families, and the love between kids and dogs. This memoir is a charmer.

Wendy Welch, author of *The Little Bookstore of Big Stone Gap*

Alison Hodgson's tender lament in the wake of her family's house fire rings with faith and hope, even laughter. Her story mirrors life itself: love and beauty, complicated by grief—but never fully extinguished.

Jen Pollock Michel, author of *Christianity Today*'s 2015 Book of the Year, *Teach Us to Want*

Why is a pug so good?" So a little girl ponders in the pages of her journal while her family rebuilds following an inexplicable and devastating loss. The answer to this simple but deeply theological question is unfolded through this riveting and delightful memoir, encompassing everything that really matters: faith, family, and the unfailing goodness of God in the midst of both suffering and joy.

Karen Swallow Prior, PhD, author of *Booked: Literature in the Soul of Me* and *Fierce Convictions: The Extraordinary Life of Hannah More—Poet, Reformer, Abolitionist*

The Pug List is the best kind of book: heartwarming and hilarious and everything in between. In her family's wrenching story of loss and discovery, Alison Hodgson reminds us that even in the worst bits of life, God stands ready to restore and redeem. And that this redemption is all the better when it comes with a dog.

Caryn Rivadeneira, author of *Known and Loved: 52 Devotions from the Psalms*

Alison Hodgson's *The Pug List* is an affecting story of the author's experience as a person of faith, a victim of arson, a present wife and mother, and a lover of dogs, who sometimes—in desperation—finds herself praying in all capital letters. And it's an account of God's mysterious, loving answers to her prayers.

Jennifer Grant, author of *Disquiet Time* and *Wholehearted Living*

What if a ludicrous little dog was the capstone for a family rebuilding—not their physical house, but their feeling of home and haven? What if he was the sneezing, wheezing answer to their prayers? In this tenderly wrought memoir, Alison Hodgson brings wisdom, spirit, and laughter to the story of what happened to her family after an arsonist set fire to their home. Anyone who has ever suffered devastation and loss or loved an animal with their whole heart will find a kindred soul in Alison, her family, and Oliver the Pug too.

Lorilee Craker, author of *Anne of Green Gables, My Daughter, and Me: What My Favorite Book Taught Me about Grace, Redemption, and the Orphan in Us All* and the *New York Times* bestseller *Through the Storm* with Lynne Spears

The
Pug List

The Pug List

A Ridiculous Little Dog, a Family
Who Lost Everything, and How They
All Found Their Way Home

ALISON HODGSON

ZONDERVAN

The Pug List
Copyright © 2016 by Alison Hodgson

Requests for information should be addressed to:
Zondervan, 3900 *Sparks Dr. SE, Grand Rapids, Michigan* 49546

ISBN 978-0-310-34605-0 (audio edition)

ISBN 978-0-310-34384-4 (ebook)

Library of Congress Cataloging-in-Publication Data

Names: Alison Hodgson, author.
Title: The pug list : a ridiculous little dog, a family who lost everything, and how they all
    found their way home / Alison Hodgson
Description: Grand Rapids, Michigan : Zondervan, 2016. | "This title is also available as a
    Zondervan ebook"—Title page verso.
Identifiers: LCCN 2015039585 | ISBN 9780310343837 (softcover)
Subjects: LCSH: Hodgson, Alison. | Hodgson, Alison—Family. | Hodgson, Alison—Homes
    and haunts. | Dwellings—Fire and fire prevention—United States. | Arson—United
    States. | Pug—United States—Biography. | Puppies—United States—Biography. |
    Human-animal relationships—United States. | Healing—United States. | Christian
    biography—United States.
Classification: LCC CT275.H6283465 A3 2016 | DDC 636.76—dc 23 LC record available at
    http://lccn.loc.gov/2015039585

Published in association with the Books & Such Literary Agency, 52 Mission Circle, Suite
122, PMB 170, Santa Rosa, California 95409-5370, www.booksandsuch.com.

Cover design: James W. Hall IV
Cover photography: Dan Davis Photography
Interior design: Kait Lamphere

First Printing February 2016 / Printed in the United States of America

This is for my husband, Paul;
and our own trinity—Christopher, Lydia, and Eden;
and for Hope, who was always in the story.

There are some who would argue that a dog's life is insignificant. But God so often chooses to use insignificant things in significant ways. In the grand scheme, we're all insignificant until love shows up.

Linford Detweiler

Contents

one

Before

The day before an arsonist set my house on fire, I had a long list of things to do.

I had books to return, plants to buy, groceries to shop for, paint to pick up, and Goodwill donations to drop off. Those were just the errands. I needed to edge and mulch our many garden beds, plant annuals, divide perennials, and paint the east side of the house. Oh—and there was laundry. There's always laundry.

I know that makes me sound incredibly industrious and organized. To be honest, when I wake up—almost every morning—I just want to stay in bed and read. Many Saturdays, that's exactly what I do, but I had been on a six-month odyssey of getting my house in order. I had gone room by room, decluttering and organizing, winnowing our possessions to only those I decided we could not live without.

The right-hand stall of our garage piled with all the things nice enough to donate was dedicated to Goodwill; the other stall was reserved for trash. My husband, Paul, had been hauling things to Goodwill and setting out extra bags of trash week after week. In the beginning, he kept up, but as I gained momentum, he couldn't keep my pace. We had been parking both of our cars in the driveway for several weeks now.

It's terrible there's no way to know your house is about to burn down, because if there was ever a day to ignore my lengthy to-do list and stay in bed reading, this was it. If, like Superman, I could fly around the earth backward in time, I would be sure to tell Day-Before-the-Fire Alison, "Hey, don't worry about it. You can just relax. Trust me." Better yet, I'd cut to the chase: "Lock the car door."

Unfortunately I'm no Superman.

I decided to run my errands first. Walking out to my van, I found my seven-year-old daughter Eden in the driveway, holding a small cardboard box.

"Look, Mama. I found a baby bird!"

All three of my children are animal lovers, with an extra tenderness reserved for abandoned creatures. For years, we had run an informal animal rescue—although it would have been more rightly called a hospice, since no animal actually survived. Eden was only one when she spotted a tree frog with a cut on its back. Her big brother and sister, Christopher and Lydia, gave the frog all their loving attention, but he only made it a couple days. This did not deter Eden. In the ensuing years, she helped provide palliative care for countless toads, several more frogs, and most notably, a young mouse she named Winkie.

They discovered Winkie creeping beside our pool. He was obviously sick and had almost certainly been abandoned to die, but the children just swung into rescue mode, gathering a cardboard box, rags, rubber gloves, and droppers. Despite hours of tender care and many prayers, Winkie didn't make it through the night.

Eden took it hard. For a week she cried herself to sleep. "He died so young. He had his whole life ahead of him!"

That was a year ago, practically to the day. I so didn't want to go through that again, but here she was—clutching yet another cardboard box. I peered inside and saw the tiniest pink thing cradled in a nest of toilet paper, so small and fragile, with eyes pinched shut, the only sign of life the barely perceptible pulse of the weakest heartbeat.

My stomach lurched.

How do you tell a child, "This is a waste of time. It's a hopeless cause. The bird is going to die anyway"?

I looked at Eden, her face shining with hope and compassion. I set my purse down beside the van. "We better sterilize the eye droppers."

While she did that, I Googled "what to feed a baby bird." Eden had so much experience that it wasn't long before she was settled, and I was able to take off.

I returned several hours later. As I unloaded the flowers, I heard the mower stop, and my husband, Paul, came around the corner pushing it. At six foot six, he's hard to miss, and while he's handsome, it's the inherent kindness in his face that you're likely to notice first. We began dating in high school, and there are moments when I can't believe we have become adults—long-married, with three kids and a lawn mower, let alone the house attached to the lawn requiring it.

"Mowing's done," he said. "I feel like going for a swim before the sun gets too low." The pool was one of the main reasons we bought this house, and while the kids were in it almost every day, Paul and I tended to spend more time maintaining it, but lately we were trying to enjoy it too.

He wheeled the mower into the garage, right next to the big red gas can, and then went inside to change. I looked at the twin towers of trash and donations. I could haul another load to Goodwill. But then I could also plant flowers or edge a garden bed or open up a can of paint and start on the east side of the house—I was itching to do that. I could make dinner. And yes, there was still laundry.

Through the clamoring of the many things I needed to do, including the few I actually wanted to do, I felt a pause I have learned to regard. I didn't want to swim, but I felt compelled to go relax with Paul. I knew I should. I went inside and poured a glass of lemonade. I whistled for Jack, our big black Lab, and he followed me outside. Paul was already in the pool. Kicking off my flip-flops, I dropped into a chaise, and Jack lay down on the patio.

Eden was soon at my side with her bird box.

"Mama, would you feed Max so I can swim with Daddy?"

It almost always comes down to the mother.

"Sure," I said, and she ran to change.

Peering into the box, I saw a little mouth open wide.

Max (I guess that's what we were calling him) had miraculously transformed into the cutest little bird. He was tiny but perfectly formed, with soft and fluffy feathers. He was also cheeping loudly.

I drizzled gruel into his gaping mouth.

I sipped my drink and watched Eden swim with Paul. Christopher joined them and for once chose not to tease his sister and just swam happily. Eventually the kids got out and went into the house. Soon it would be time to pick up Lydia from a middle-school-age church camping trip, but not just yet.

The sun fell behind the tree line on our hill, casting long shadows on the lawn. It was still June. The grass was lush and a shade of green so rich that it almost hurt. It was the time of day photographers refer to as "magic hour."

Paul came to the edge of the pool, and we talked. I looked over the fence to the side yard that stretched to the woods—the side yard I had big plans for. I have this tendency to focus on what's missing and not see everything that is. But that evening, despite the fact that I hadn't planted any of the annuals or mulched or even edged any of the garden beds, all I could see was the beauty.

Except for the persistent cheeping of Max, whom I continued to feed, dropper by dropper, it was quiet, and I felt utterly at peace.

Who could imagine that in a matter of hours, a stranger would steal into our garage and set our house—our life—on fire? Who could know that a clock was ticking, that sand was slipping, that even as I am tipping back my head to savor the last drops in my glass, we are all drinking the last of our life before the fire?

two

It Only Takes a Spark
—and an Arsonist with a Can Full of Gas—
to Get a Fire Going

I opened my eyes and saw a figure standing beside the bed—a small, dark figure.

"Mama," Eden whispered, "I'm scared."

"Abracadabra-Doo?" I asked, and she nodded.

A few weeks before, she had watched an episode of *Scooby-Doo* that showed, in the credits, wallpaper patterned with black widow spiders crawling up the walls.

"The episode didn't scare me," she had made clear, "just those spiders." She hadn't slept well since. This was not her first early-morning visit.

I lifted the duvet. She snuggled between Paul and me. I stroked her hair and kissed her head. Within minutes, she flopped over and was half-asleep. I was wide-awake.

I got up to go to the bathroom and checked on Max, who was just outside my bedroom. Lifting up the towel that Eden had partially covered his box with to keep him warm, I listened and couldn't hear breathing. I sighed. I didn't want to go another round of mourning with Eden, but a mom gets to do what her kid needs her to do. I crawled back into bed and fumbled in the dark for the book I had been reading the night before and turned on my Itty Bitty Book Light.

It wasn't long before I noticed a peculiar, hot smell, and I worried the bulb on my book light was burning out. I didn't have a backup bulb, and I didn't want to wake up Paul by turning on my bedside lamp. An insomniac without her trusty book light is like a tightrope walker without a net. I returned to my book. Nero fiddled; I read.

Paul turned over, and I froze. We both looked at the clock. It was 4:39. He noticed Eden. "When did she show up?"

I shrugged.

He sniffed. "What's that smell?"

"I think it's my Itty Bitty Book Light." I waited for him to ask me to turn it off.

"That's not your book light." He threw back the covers, pulled on a pair of shorts and a shirt, and headed for the door. I got up too. I wasn't worried, but Paul and I are a team, and I wanted to help.

I hadn't even reached the doorway when the smoke alarms began blaring.

"It's just the alarms, honey. Stay here," I told Eden, who shot up, fully awake. "I'll be right back."

Our alarm system was wired throughout the house, and the racket was so loud that I felt it in my chest, but I was annoyed rather than scared. My first thought was of Hope, our twelve-year-old daughter Lydia's friend, who was sleeping over. The girls had been away on a church trip the day before, and Hope was spending the rest of the weekend with us while her parents were away.

Worst sleepover ever, I thought, as the alarms whooped and shrilled.

I had no idea.

Lydia and Hope spilled out of the bedroom, and Eden trailed out of ours. We huddled together outside the mudroom, where the security control panel for the alarm was and watched Paul try to shut it off. Despite the wailing alarms, neither one of us could imagine that our house was actually on fire. We'd had false alarms before—burnt toast, too much steam. Even *thinking* about turning on the oven seemed to set off our old system. The fire chief once stopped by to tell us that when they see our address come up at the station, they ignore the call and wait for it to be canceled.

"You don't want us to ignore your house," he said, and we agreed. The security company came out and updated the system. That was more than a year ago, and we'd had no trouble since.

Paul entered the code, and the alarms stopped. We exhaled. Now to call and report a false alarm—and figure out that smell. There was the lightest haze in the air, but I'd had more smoke from a pepperoni falling off a pizza and burning on the bottom of my oven. I was sure there was some benign explanation.

"Christopher," I said, looking at Paul.

Christopher is our oldest child and only son. He was born deaf and can only hear through the processor of his cochlear implant. He sleeps without it and is a deep and sound sleeper anyway who likes to cover his head with blankets. Since he was a toddler, he's been impossibly hard to wake.

Paul and I had the same thought. The second story of our house was one large room and mainly the children's area. During the school year, we had strict restrictions on video games and screen time in general, but it was summer, and Christopher, fourteen, had been staying up till all hours playing games, watching movies, or reading as late as he liked. A couple times, he had fallen asleep on one of the sofas or on the floor.

We both imagined him curled up under a blanket with a lamp knocked over, melting the carpet. Christopher accidentally destroying something was within our understanding. Someone setting our house on fire? Not on the radar.

Paul ran upstairs to check.

I turned to the girls. "Stay here." Then I ran after Paul.

He stood in the middle of the room and looked around. I waited on the landing at the top of the stairs, wanting to be there to help but also to stay within sight of the girls. But we could both see the room was empty.

The room in which we were standing was over the garage, where— although we didn't know it yet—the fire had started. It was burning directly below us. In a matter of minutes, this floor would be gone, and only a skeleton of the stairs would remain. Paul opened one of the doors to the storage area, and the haze thickened. Again the alarms began to blare.

"We need to get out, babe," I said. I was clear on this, and yet I didn't really believe the house was on fire. I pictured us huddled on the pavement, the fire trucks coming to find some small electrical problem—one big misunderstanding. We would look ridiculous and feel embarrassed, I was sure, but better safe than sorry.

Paul stared back for a moment. "OK, let's go."

"I'll get Christopher. You get the girls and find Jack." Both our boys, human and canine, needed to be accounted for.

I ran downstairs through the mudroom, dining room, and kitchen, down the little hall to Christopher's room. Although I wasn't conscious of it, I was following a plan I had made years before.

Even with the peculiar layout of our house, the bedrooms were all close together, except for Christopher's small bedroom. When we considered room assignments, I hesitated placing any of the children here, especially Christopher because of his hearing. But it had a built-in bed with bookshelves. We hung heavy curtains, and he was able to cocoon in utter darkness. He loved it, but I was concerned about him being down that little hall.

Having a child with special needs heightened what almost certainly would have been a propensity for maternal anxiety, and as our family grew, so did my fears. I had more I needed to protect. Paul worked in the international division of his company's legal department and traveled frequently for work. When he was gone, I felt vulnerable and found myself preparing for emergencies and planning evacuations. A fire was the most easily imagined disaster.

What would we do? I thought through every scenario—if we had access to all the bedrooms, or if some were blocked. I considered what I would do if it was just the kids and me: First I would wake up the girls and charge Lydia with Eden's care, then run to wake up Christopher. If I couldn't get down the hall, I would make my way outside and even break his window if necessary. I had pictured myself clawing at the screen and breaking the glass. Something I read suggested establishing a meeting point. I talked with the children about it. We decided on the red maple at the front of our property, right by the road.

"This will probably never happen," I told the children. "But it's good to be prepared."

I opened Christopher's door and saw Jack sleeping across the foot of the bed. He jumped off and ran out of the room. At first I couldn't see

Christopher under his mound of heavy quilts. I patted the bed and was relieved to feel his leg.

I pulled back the blankets and shook him awake. He can barely hear without his processor and relies on lipreading when it's off.

"Get up!" I mouthed. He stared, bleary-eyed. He was wearing only his boxers, so I looked around for shorts. His dresser drawers were stuffed and overflowing onto the floor. I grabbed a pair of shorts and turned. He had fallen back asleep. I shook him again and shoved the shorts at him. He sat up and languidly stretched one leg. I bent down to paw through the pile of clothes on his floor in search of a shirt. I looked up, and he was slumped sideways, asleep.

It was like the Marx brothers, but not one bit funny. The alarms continued to whoop and wail, creating a sense of urgency. My heart was pounding. I smacked Christopher's leg hard, and his eyes snapped open.

"We have to go! GET UP!"

He fumbled for his processor and fit it over his ear.

"Can you hear the alarms?" I asked. "We need to get out."

He staggered out of bed.

I handed him the shorts, and he pulled them on. I grabbed his arm to drag him out the door, and he pulled away.

"I need to get my—"

"No!" I pushed him out the door and up the hall, through the kitchen, and into the dining room, where the girls had gathered with Paul. Lydia had Jack on the leash, and Hope stood wide-eyed beside them. Eden clutched the box where Max the sparrow was sleeping or dead.

Paul was on the phone with 911. He walked into the entryway, and the children lined up behind him like ducklings. One by one, they ran out the front door. For a moment, I was alone in the dining room and looked around. What if my house was actually on fire? I knew it wasn't, of course. *But what if it is?* I wondered. *What should I take?* I thought of my laptop sitting just steps away on the desk in my study. I slid it into the bag that was sitting on the floor right next to the desk. I didn't even take the time to unplug the cord.

I was sure we'd be right back.

three

Fight or Flight

We all have these key moments when everything shifts and life is forever divided. We go about our days with the illusion we are in control until something happens, the veil is torn away, and it's suddenly so clear we are not. So often, we only recognize it in hindsight.

On my desk sits a tiny teacup. The outside is painted my favorite green that falls smack between the brightness of grass and the softness of a piece of jadeite. The handle and inside are a deep sky blue, at least they once were. The paint has chipped or simply worn off in patches, and ash has blackened the upper edge of the brim and almost the entire inner bowl. It is the sole survivor of a "paint your own" set given to Lydia the Christmas she was five. I keep it as a talisman of Before.

The set was a gift from her aunt and uncle—my sister, Torey, and her husband, David—who were visiting for the holidays. The day after Christmas, Lydia invited everyone to help her paint. We were gathered around the table when the call came from my mother. She was at the hospital with my father. He had been suffering for weeks from what he self-diagnosed as a bad case of bronchitis. Concerned, I talked to a friend—an actual doctor—and she suspected congestive heart failure. At my insistence, my dad scheduled an appointment with a cardiologist on December 26. They took one look and immediately admitted him to the hospital.

My family, along with Torey and David, had spent the day there with him, but Mom sent us home to have dinner. We planned to visit the next morning. Torey and I were both pregnant, and knowing surgery was imminent, we were trying to pace ourselves.

Just my mother was there when the surgeon stopped by on evening rounds with the news that Dad's heart damage was so bad that reparative surgery might not be an option. A transplant might be his only hope.

I held the phone to my ear, disbelieving. My mother's words surreal.

And just like that, my father's immortality, in my eyes at least, was shattered. It would be six more months, half of them spent in the ICU, before he would actually die, but this moment was the beginning of the end. I didn't recognize it at the time, but in the same swift moment I hung up the phone, I crossed the threshold from the Before to the After.

I called my mother-in-law to come over to watch Christopher, and then Lydia, Paul, David, Torey, and I rushed to the hospital, the tea set entirely forgotten.

Four years later, another hospital—this time it was just Paul and I with Lydia, who had symptoms of appendicitis. While we waited for the results of her CT scan, Paul and I didn't speak, but we were both thinking the same thing. It was April, and Lydia was ten years old. Christopher was twelve. The April when Paul was twelve, he had a persistent cough that didn't go away until finally his mother took him to the doctor, who gave the diagnosis of non-Hodgkin's lymphoma, and Paul's life changed forever.

When your children reach the age you were when you experienced a traumatic event, it's common, on one level, to relive it with this beloved embodiment of your younger self. Early in the month, when Christopher caught a cold, Paul and I were both on edge. We prayed and kept an especially close eye. Christopher recovered quickly, and we were relieved, but the same foreboding returned as we waited for Lydia's test results in the hospital.

The chalky drink she took before the CT scan made her sick, and a kind nurse had prepared a bed in the large recovery area. We were the only ones there. Lydia was quiet and resting. Paul and I sat on either side of her bed, both of us hoping she had appendicitis.

What sort of parents would hope this? We didn't, not really. We hoped it was nothing, but we already knew it was *something*, and appendicitis was something manageable. I tried not to think of any other possibilities.

I was acutely aware we might be straddling a Before and After. It felt like we were on a precipice, and this was the first time I recognized it right in the moment. If Lydia had appendicitis, we would remain in life as Before—life as it was supposed to be. Appendicitis can be treated; I knew Lydia—and Paul and I—would survive it. There wouldn't be a

Before or After; there would just be the glorious now. Life as we knew it would continue.

The nurse returned with the news—it was, in fact, appendicitis. A surgeon would meet with us shortly. As we told Lydia, I began to cry from relief, but the nurse misunderstood.

"You're going to be just fine," she told Lydia. "We'll be getting you into surgery right away, and you'll be better before you know it."

"Mom," she said to me in an undertone, "we need to stay calm."

Although I was trying to stay calm, I have never thought crying was necessarily at odds with that. For my children, seeing me cry was as normal as breathing, and these were tears of joy!

What sorts of parents are thrilled their child has appendicitis? The sort who have been through worse.

Lydia's surgery went smoothly. She was home and well on the road to healing the very next day. That time, we weren't thrust into After, but something still changed for me, and I didn't forget. I ruminated on how we have these key moments when everything shifts and life divides. The next time I came across that little green and blue teacup, I recognized it for what it was: a souvenir of the last moments before my dad's long and arduous death. I tucked it in the top drawer of my nightstand, where it remained until a friend found it during one of our searches through the ruins after the fire.

She held it up. "Is this important?"

I grabbed it.

"Yes," I said. "It's important."

I was the last one out of the house.

Our cars were parked in the driveway, and the driver's side door on Paul's was standing open. I stopped at the end of our front walk and couldn't see it, but Paul did when he ran past. He stood in the doorway of the far garage stall and peered inside. The garage door was up, and I saw the orange glow of flames on the wall.

Our house was truly on fire. Finally I was confronted with the proof. And still, I couldn't believe it.

It didn't occur to me to wonder why the garage door was up. Paul noticed his car door open and the garage door that was raised. One of the last things he had done the night before was check that the garage doors were down when he locked the back door. He knew the fire wasn't an accident. I was in shock, but he was in fix-it mode and had been since the alarms started to blare.

"I saw that the garage door was up and wanted to see exactly what was burning," he would later explain. "If it had been something small enough, I planned to haul it out of the garage and extinguish it on the lawn, but the flames were already too big."

This is the story he told over and over in the early days. Most men listening nodded in agreement. Of course you'd grab something on fire—with your bare hands—and try to put it out. Any guy would. It's your *home*.

Almost every woman hearing this looked at me, and I simply raised an eyebrow to acknowledge, "Yes, my sister, I hear the crazy talk."

The fire was already too big, and Paul knew it had grown beyond his power to control. He turned away, and without a word, the rest of us followed. We ran to the edge of the yard and gathered under the large maple, just as I had planned so long ago. We faced the house, and I tried to catch my breath. For the first time, I saw the actual flames. They were reaching up and out of the garage, igniting the power lines running across our yard and above our heads. I could hear them crackle and knew we had to get farther away.

"We gotta move," Paul said.

We turned as one person and lined up at the edge of the road, about to cross the street, when I saw the shine of headlights.

We live at the cross section of two busy roads, but woods and fields separate many of the houses, and our closest neighbor is a small hobby farm across the street. It was not quite five on a Sunday morning, a time when our road is silent. I was barefoot, standing in the gravel between Eden and Christopher, clutching their hands, waiting for the car to crest the hill and then turn left or right at the intersection. I could feel our collective tension; we all stood on the razor's edge of adrenaline: FLIGHT! FLIGHT! FLIGHT! We yearned to run. But even in that moment, I saw the ridiculousness of the idea of getting hit by a car, having just escaped our burning house. Safety first.

The car stopped at the stop sign, and we waited. Left or right? Left or right? I felt like a sprinter poised on the block, everything in me straining for the starter shot. The door opened, and the driver staggered into the intersection. We were transfixed. He pulled out his phone, and I couldn't tell if he was taking a picture or texting. Paul and I looked at each other, incredulous. Neither of us could believe this knucklehead was mucking up our evacuation. We nodded in agreement that it was safe to cross. All six of us fanned out, and I was on the edge closest to the intersection. I stared at the driver, who was about ten feet away. He looked to be in his early twenties, dark hair, phone in hand. He looked up, and when our eyes met, he startled.

"Is that your house?" he called out loudly from across the road.

Ladies and gentlemen, here's the man of the hour. Meet our arsonist.

Of course, I didn't know it then. I had only just barely accepted the fact that our house was actually on fire. Mentally, I had not even gotten that far to question what—or who—might be at fault. I thought he was just some clueless kid asking the stupidest question anyone had ever asked me.

This is where it became clear to me there were proprieties to consider, even in the midst of an emergency. This is where I first established the idea of "Fire Etiquette."

Fire Don'ts: *Don't rudely interrupt a family's escape from their burning home to take pictures and ask "Captain Obvious" questions.*

I was already annoyed with him for making us wait, and now I couldn't believe his bad manners.

I had no idea.

Later, when I tell the story, I will riff on possible replies:

"Oh no, it's the neighbor's house, and we got the children up to watch!"

"We're just out for an early morning run . . . in our pajamas . . . with the kids . . . and the dog . . . and this sparrow!"

Or the real kicker: "No! We just set it on fire and are fleeing the scene!"

I was too astonished to speak, let alone make smart-aleck remarks. As it was, "GAAAAAAAAH!" seemed the only reasonable response, so that's exactly what I said as I pulled Eden and Christopher across the road to the bike path where Paul and the girls were standing.

None of us noted when he got back in his car and drove away. We were too busy trying to take it all in—huddled together, watching our house burn. It's just what you do—arsonist and victims alike, whether or not you know it.

One of the first things I noticed was how fast the fire was moving; I couldn't have imagined how quickly it could spread. I willed the fire trucks to arrive. I felt anxious and strangely embarrassed, with this inexplicable sense of wrongdoing—as if it was a big mess we had made, and it was all our fault. *If only the fire trucks would get here and put out the fire*, I thought, *then Paul and I can clean things up.* I remembered the fire chief's warning about our old and faulty alarm and prayed they weren't ignoring this one.

A sheriff's car pulled up, and Paul stepped over to the open window. "The trucks are on their way," the sheriff said. "Is there anyone I can call?" Paul gave him his sister Dawn's number.

Within minutes, the fire trucks began to arrive from all directions. By then, the fire had burned through the roof and was reaching to the treetops. Through our glass front door, I could see into our dining room. It shared a wall with the garage, and I could see it lit by the orange glow of the fire burning but not yet all the way through. The second story was in flames, but because the fire hadn't yet spread outside the garage on the first floor, it still seemed contained. I prayed they could stop it before the house was consumed.

Television trucks arrived, and the bright lights of cameras were trained on the fire. I stiffened at the thought of giving an interview. I didn't want to be that pathetic and befuddled family on the side of the road. That may have been exactly what we were, but I didn't want it captured on film. A man with a newspaper press badge set up a tripod just down the path and took a few pictures. He carefully walked in front of us, and his eye met mine before he glanced away. It was clear he was trying not to intrude.

I heard the soft sound of a strange, yet familiar beeping. I looked around and saw Paul bent over the cordless phone from which he called 911 as he ran out of the house. Now the phone was giving the alert it was still on. I watched as Paul pushed a button again and again, but it wouldn't turn off because it was too far from the base.

Paul is an "i" dotter and a "t" crosser. Paul takes care of things. He wraps up cords, zips zippers, shuts doors; he assesses and tries to extinguish literal and figurative fires. He turns off phones, unless they refuse to be turned off. I knew this was killing him.

Often, even in terrible crises, the only way to alleviate another's suffering is to remove the seemingly small irritants that loom right in front of that person. We don't know this yet, but this will be the key to surviving everything.

"If you take out the battery, it may stop the beeping," I said.

He did, and it worked.

Later we will laugh at how he could have just thrown the phone back into the fire, but true to his nature, Paul slipped it into his pocket for safekeeping.

"I'm so sorry." This was Hope. I turned to look at her. Her lovely hazel eyes were huge. I have known her since she was a baby. She and Lydia are each other's oldest friend and can't remember life without the other.

"I'm so sorry," Hope murmured again, clutching Max's box, which Eden had handed her as soon as we reached the path.

Hope was thirteen years old—in the midst of a terrible trauma and separated from her parents, yet sensitive enough to recognize this was not her tragedy. She tried to delicately separate herself and offer comfort. She was trying to do the right thing too.

"I'm so sorry," she said yet again, and I smiled.

"I'm sorry I keep saying I'm sorry . . . I just don't know what to say."

"It's OK," I said, putting my arm around her. "It's our first fire too." We laughed at the terrible strangeness of everything.

I slowly breathed in and out like I learned in a birthing class long ago and have made my go-to in every painful situation since. But I didn't feel any pain and was surprised by its absence. My subconscious,

Rolodex-like, had already flicked through my history of hard times, trying to place this unbelievable experience: the untimely death of my father, Christopher's multiple and protracted diagnoses, my own depression, the loss of my childhood home in the aftermath of the massive embezzlement of our family business, and the loss of my childhood itself with the death of Paul's father to suicide when Paul and I were high school sweethearts.

Paul and I had certainly had our share of trying times. We were no stranger to the Before and After moments.

Then, glimpsing between the firefighters, the reporters, and the smoke, I saw flames burning through the front door and knew that was that: All was lost. I knew we didn't live there anymore, but it still didn't hurt. It was like touching a bruise, anticipating the involuntary wince and feeling nothing.

Call it survivor instinct, call it coping, call it grace—I was clearer than I've ever been: What was burning was merely stuff, and it could be replaced. My family, there beside me, alive and physically unharmed, was irreplaceable. I took in another deep breath and let it out. It was well with my soul.

I can take this, I thought, and I was suffused with relief.

How could I know that losing everything is only the beginning with a house fire?

Christopher was next to me, silent but with tears streaming down his face. I reached out to pat his back and then put my arm around his shoulders and pulled him close. He sagged against me.

"I sure am glad I opened my bank account," Eden said. She had climbed into Paul's arms, and her little face was serious but calm. For weeks, she had been begging to go to the bank to open a savings account for her Pug Fund, as she called it. We had talked about adopting another dog, and she had saved all her money for weeks. Someone else had just adopted the particular pug we had our eye on, but Eden was undeterred and eager to open a formal savings account. Sweet girl with her little bit of money—almost nothing to us but everything to her—and I was happy she had this small comfort.

By then, flames were burning through all the windows on the front of the house, and Lydia realized the fire had surely reached her room. She turned to face Hope, both arms outstretched.

"Hope!" she said, arms swinging back to the house and gesturing like a model on *The Price Is Right* toward a most terrible showcase showdown. "All your stuff!" Only twelve, she was ever the excellent hostess.

Hope looked at Lydia, surprised. With one hand, she panned the entire scene. "Lydia, your HOUSE!" Oh, perfect and wonderful guest.

Paul gave the sheriff the phone number of his sister Dawn as someone in the area who could help. She was still sleeping when the phone rang. She really only heard the sheriff say something about a house on Red Cedar Drive and told him, "No, I don't have a house on Red Cedar." She and her husband, Thom, own many rental houses, and being not fully awake, she thought that's what the call was about.

"It's Paul's," Thom said.

"What?" Dawn asked.

"He's calling about Paul's house."

"My brother lives on Red Cedar," Dawn said. She thought the sheriff said there was a garage fire and that we needed a ride. She promised they would be right there.

Thom asked about taking both cars, but Dawn figured Paul and I would be sticking around to deal with things and only needed them to take the kids. One car would be fine. When they crested our hill, the house was engulfed in flames reaching beyond the treetops.

"That's not a garage fire!" she screeched.

The road was blocked. Dawn explained to the sheriff on duty that they were there to pick us up. He told them to park and walk down to get us.

"Get them out of here," he said. "They don't need to see this."

In a matter of minutes, Paul and I had shifted from capable and competent adults to people standing by the side of the road in need of rescue, and whether or not we realized it, we were living After the Fire. I didn't notice the moment we moved past Before. Even now I couldn't tell you exactly when we crossed the line from one to the other. Did our autonomy end as soon as the match was lit? When the alarms began to sound? Was it when Paul realized he couldn't extinguish the fire? When I saw the flames burning through our front door? Or was it when the sheriff told Dawn to take us away—all of us, no distinctions for adults—because Paul and I could stand to be shielded and protected too.

I turned back and saw Dawn and Thom walking toward us. Thom's face was set, almost stern. Dawn was visibly breathing in through her nose and out through her mouth, slowly and deeply—obviously trying to pull herself together. I noticed this, but it was all so distant. I could feel her emotions, but they didn't make sense. We were fine. Fine. There was no need to be upset.

A light, almost spitting rain was just beginning to fall, and we followed Dawn and Thom back to their SUV, where for a moment I hesitated about the seat belts—there weren't enough for all of us. I won't drive a block if my kids aren't buckled up. But then the rain intensified, and Paul said it would be fine. We piled in. Paul, Eden, and I climbed into the backseat, and the big kids crawled into the trunk area with Jack.

As we drove away, I didn't think to look back.

four

Fire Etiquette

Later, when I need to reference the fire and want to succinctly explain what happened, I simply say, "When an arsonist randomly set our house on fire, we were all home and in bed, and we escaped with the clothes on our backs."

And there, in a mere twenty-five words, you have the story. Not the whole story, of course, but you get the gist. So what does the casual observer learn? The fire wasn't an accident, but neither was it personal. One word, *randomly*, tells you the arsonist didn't know us. You also gather that it happened in the early hours and that no one was killed or physically injured, and it explains we lost everything. Those twenty-five words pack a lot, but it's hard to tell any story—let alone a whole one—in just a sentence. One of the things that bugs me most about this super-condensed version is that it leaves out Hope.

When we arrived at Dawn and Thom's, my kids quickly settled in to a semipeaceful state. Going to Aunt Dawn and Uncle Thom's was always a treat. This was practically their second home.

For Hope, of course, nothing was familiar. Once we left the fire, her first reserves of strength flagged. She wanted her mom and dad. She and Lydia stepped into Dawn's office to make the call. Hope's parents were on a rare getaway attending a family wedding and had turned off their phones. They never turned off their phones, but just this once they did. Hope called and called. No answer. She began to panic but tried to stay calm and just kept calling.

I was oblivious to all of this. I mean, I knew she was trying to reach her parents, but I wasn't thinking about her feelings; I was thinking about logistics. We could stick with the original plan of a sleepover—or a "slightly" amended version of it. Hope was welcome to stay with us. I had no idea she was scared. Having just awoken to a near-death experience, of course, this makes complete sense. A fire has a way of disorienting—well—everything.

Finally she reached an aunt, who knew the name of the hotel and was able to contact Hope's parents on the other side of the state, more than two hours away. More calls were made, and a close family friend offered to drive out to Dawn's to pick up Hope. She would keep her until Hope's parents arrived. They were already on their way home, and I didn't understand why any of this was necessary.

When the family friend arrived, she was in tears. I hugged her. "Yes, it's terrible, but we're fine. We're OK. We're going to be OK," I assured her. I hugged Hope. She could have stayed—we love Hope. Still clueless about her need and fear, I knew she was leaving, but I didn't understand how much that meant. Only later would I realize how terrified she was, and I deeply regret I didn't protect her better.

In the future, I will have to forgive myself. Eventually I will decide to give myself a break. I don't know anyone who would be on her A game the day someone sets her house on fire. I was clueless and in shock, doing the best I was capable of, and I had my own calls to make. I started with my mother.

"Mom," I said and paused. I hadn't yet said it out loud. How do you even tell someone your house burned down? I felt like I was about to pull the pin and lob a hand grenade.

"There's just no good way to say it: Our house burned down." Now that I think about it, this was the first version I told, and it would remain the simplest. It was incomplete, and not entirely accurate, but it would do for breaking the news.

"WHAT!"

And then I told her about our escape and that we were all safe at Dawn and Thom's, and she said she would come up right after church.

I called my sister next. Telling my mother didn't make this second round any easier. I stuck to the basics.

Her reaction was pretty much the same as Mom's, but then Torey pulled herself together.

"OK. OK. I would come right over, but I'm volunteering at church this morning. I'll come up to Dawn's as soon as we're out."

I said that was fine. We were fine. We would talk later. A minute later, the phone rang.

"I don't know what I was thinking. I'm not going to church."

"OK. Whatever you think is best."

"Do you want me to go to the store for you? You need—everything. OK, I'm going to get the girls up, then we'll head to Target and get you some toiletries and underwear and an outfit for each of you, although that may be tricky with Paul."

Paul is so tall that I have been shopping for him almost exclusively online for years.

"He's wearing shorts and a shirt. So he's OK for today."

"What about shoes? Does everyone have a pair?"

"I don't. I grabbed my laptop instead."

"Oh, thank God, you got your computer."

"I know. It's the only thing I took. I didn't bother to get dressed. I'm wearing pajamas. I don't even have a bra."

"I'll try to buy you a bra, and I'll definitely pick you up a pair of flip-flops."

After the fire was put out, the fire chief called us back to the house to interview us for his report. Dawn rooted through her closet to find me something to wear. I had on my cutest pajamas, a fact that brought me a measure of comfort as we stood on the path and watched the house burn. If you have to evacuate your house in the wee hours of the morning, it's nice to look your best.

Dawn and I couldn't be built more differently, so she turned to her workout clothes to cobble together an outfit. The ensemble we came up with was an XL T-shirt from a 5K in an eye-searing hot pink and some Lycra leggings that hit me mid-calf and were—oh, the humanity—white. Shoes were tricky, but we settled on a pair of silver sandals two sizes too big. After I got dressed, we laughed. All I needed was a super-high ponytail, some enormous hoop earrings, and a wad of gum to crack, and I would be set as captain of some terrible cheer team. I couldn't have felt any less like myself, but I was ready to go; the surrealism and leftover adrenaline in a potent mix were still pushing me forward. Dawn lent us her car, and Paul drove us back to—I didn't know what to call it any-more. *The house? The scene of the crime?* It was no longer home.

Driving the road to our house, you crest a small hill right before you reach the intersection. It had always been a good feeling—to reach the hill and first see the trees at the top of the hill behind our house and then, there ahead, our house nestled below.

Coming up over the hill now, I was filled with nervous anticipation, but I didn't know what to expect. We crested the hill, and the house came into view. My brain and my eyes tripped over each other for a few seconds until I could register what I was seeing.

Paul and I both gasped.

The garage and most of the second story had disappeared—a charred absence. My eye was drawn to the half-burned stairs that now led to nowhere. The part of the attic where Paul had searched for Christopher a couple hours before was gone—all of it, including the landing where I stood and waited, thinking there was no way our house could be on fire while standing right above it.

I could just see into the mudroom where Paul had tried, again and again, to turn off the alarm. How annoyed we had been. We thought our only worry was frightening the kids. We just wanted to shut it off, even as the fire was burning and growing mere feet behind our backs.

All of us made it out of that house safely—untouched by even a hint of ash. In this moment, I realized how easily it could have been another story. Paul or I or one of the girls could have opened the door to the garage—but I couldn't think about that.

Unbidden, an overpowering feeling arose, and for a moment, I became the embodiment of prayer. *Thank you.*

The site was a mess. How quickly it shifted—no longer home, not even a house. Our cars were burned-out shells. This was especially shocking. Beirut was my first thought. Pictures on the news from my childhood. War-torn places far, far away. But this was my house, our home. It *was.*

This was our new After. We had crossed a line we could never turn back from.

Earlier, at Dawn and Thom's, Paul had told us how he had noticed the driver's side door on his car was cocked open, and the corresponding garage door was rolled all the way up, and what he thought that indicated. So many things about that day are seared into my memory, but I only have the haziest recollection of him telling me this. My brain was struggling to process the basic fact of the fire, and that someone may have set it was so much more than too much information. In a way, I took it in stride; that it could be arson was just another layer of something I couldn't believe. Thank God for shock. I stood there calmly while Paul told the fire chief, who had met us there to survey the damage. Immediately he let out a heavy sigh. Just like that, it became a criminal investigation.

People stopped by, mostly neighbors, some I had never met. Everyone wanted to know about the children. One older woman rushed out of her car and ran across the driveway, her arms outstretched.

"Is everyone safe?" she cried out.

I felt her emotion and thought of the children. I couldn't speak and dumbly nodded.

"Thank God! Thank God!" she said and pulled me close. I was so sure we were OK, that we'd get through this, but something about this kindness from a stranger broke me. I fell into her arms sobbing, even though I had no idea who she was. She clutched me close, and I held on just as tightly. Then, as quickly as she had come, she let go and dashed back to her car. After she left, I remembered she was a distant neighbor whom Christopher and I had met once while walking Jack. Later she will return and hand me an envelope with a big, fat check in it. That's a "Fire Do" of the best variety.

Another woman pulled up along the side of the road and walked up to me and introduced herself. She was a distant neighbor who also knew my sister. She said she was so sorry.

"I wanted to do something for you, but I didn't know what." She thrust a bank envelope toward my hand. "It's only money," she said. "I'm sorry it's not more."

"Oh no," I said and snatched away my hand as if from fire. "That's not necessary. We're fine. We have savings and insurance. We'll be fine."

The illogic of this didn't occur to me. I was wearing a ridiculous outfit, and my personal wardrobe—what I actually owned—was limited to a pair of pajamas and one pair of underpants. I no longer had shoes that fit, or even a bra—which is pretty much the opposite of "fine."

"Please," she said, "I want to help." She clearly felt awkward and uncomfortable. Emily Post doesn't cover the proper way to hand cash to the displaced—and certainly not what to do when she's refusing it. I could feel her tension but had too much of my own; there's no guide for the proud and addled refugee either. She shoved the envelope into my hand.

"Thank you," I managed to choke out before she ran off, which was what I should have said from the start.

A childhood friend stopped by with her husband. They saw the house on the way to church and immediately headed home. She stuffed a bag with clothes for me and then left her husband with the baby and drove back to our place.

"You're going to need to keep notes." She handed me a pen and a small journal. Again, I resisted. *I'm the Imelda Marcos of paper*, I thought. I *was*. I remembered all my notebooks were reduced to ash and accepted hers.

"Thank you." Good girl. I was learning.

"You should call the Red Cross," she said.

I was appalled. The Red Cross was for people after a disaster—like floods, tornadoes, and hurricanes. Standing in front of my burned-out house in the getup I had on, I can't really tell you how I managed to think I didn't belong in the disaster category, but I did.

"This is exactly why they exist." She handed me the bag of clothes and hugged me good-bye.

By then, two detectives had arrived, straight out of central casting. They both had no-nonsense haircuts and wore Dockers-ish khakis with sports coats but no ties. Dark sunglasses and tough, emotionless expressions completed their look.

We were the first suspects, I learned. "Persons of interest" is the technical term for the early stage of the investigation, but I felt like a suspect.

"I'm sorry for these intrusive questions," one said apologetically. Paul and I stood together facing them.

"Are you having financial difficulties?"

"No," we both said, shaking our heads.

"Have either of you lost your job?"

"No."

"Any marital troubles? Are you considering divorce?"

"No and no."

"Do you have any enemies? Anyone you know have a grievance against you?"

"No, not that we can think of."

This was total bad manners. I knew they were just doing their jobs, and that when they checked our bank accounts and Paul's employment, everything would support what we'd said. I knew we were *innocent*, but it was terrible merely being under suspicion.

It didn't occur to me that our children were persons of interest too.

"Now about this friend—" a detective began to say. It took a moment for it to click that he was referring to Hope. I pictured her trying to offer comfort to us as the fire raged—her sweet face and her kind eyes.

Paul and I both assured the detectives that Hope is a wonderful girl, and we knew she had nothing to do with this. They suspected Lydia too and grilled us about the girls' movements the night before—if either had gone out to the garage, whether or not they were in their beds when the fire alarms went off.

I felt my face grow warmer with every question. *I* could handle being under suspicion, but the fact that those two beautiful girls, who thought only of the other's loss as our house was engulfed in flames, were even a consideration, made me sick.

I couldn't think of two girls *less* likely to set a house on fire. They had just come home from a church camping trip. They were straight-A students. They were *good* girls. But then I remembered that parents are often deluded, even though I knew I was right about these two. After my initial protestations, I shut up. It was the detectives' jobs to investigate, and it was not my responsibility to persuade them about where they were wasting their time.

Eventually the detectives released us, and we extricated ourselves from all the well-wishers and returned to Dawn's.

As we drove away, I touched Paul's hand. "I never want to get past gratitude," I said. "No matter what the future holds"—I was thinking vaguely of insurance and rebuilding—"I never want to stop being thankful."

At Dawn's house, Torey met us with bags and bags from Target. The kids were happy to try on their new clothes, and I was beyond grateful to wear something that fit. More people began to arrive. Soon it was a blur of family and friends. A friend of Dawn and Thom's brought platters of food. It almost felt like a party.

Dawn told me two representatives from the Red Cross were on their way. My friend called on our behalf, knowing I wouldn't, which bugged me. We were fine. We did not need the Red Cross. That they were willing to come, of course, should have been a sign that we did. And that we no longer had a home for them to come to should have been a clue to me that we needed all the help we could get. But I was riding high on shock and adrenaline and maybe more than a little pride.

The Red Cross women were both kind and low-key. I don't know what I expected. One of the first questions they carefully asked was whether or not we were insured. When we said we were, they visibly relaxed; their job had just gotten a lot easier. Since family had taken us in and our immediate needs were being met, they decided the best way they could help was with money for clothes. They gave us a credit/gift card and an informational pamphlet titled "After a Fire."

If there was any doubt before, there was none now. Life "Before" was gone. Life "After" had begun.

I felt great, but I knew that watching your house burn down is not good for children. I asked if they could suggest a therapist, and they said they would contact someone on our behalf.

When the therapist called that evening, I slipped away to talk. I liked her. She was calm and fully present. I asked her what I could do to help the children and what I should look for in them.

"A normal response for the child is to exhibit an exaggerated form of his or her normal personality. A loud, outgoing kid is going to be especially loud. A quiet, contemplative child is probably going to get quieter, go deep. A feeling and emotional kid is going to be really, really emotional." She told me about some red flags to be on the lookout for and wished me the best, reiterating her sympathy for our situation.

I was scribbling everything she said in my little notebook.

"Should we let the children see the house?" Half of it, including all the bedrooms, was still standing.

"I would let each child decide for themselves. Let their wishes guide you." My inclination was to shield them from the sight of our home in ruins, but this made sense.

"Do you know a therapist who specializes in house fires?"

"Anyone who is trained in grief and loss will be able to help you."

I didn't know how to say it or how to ask for help. But what I really wanted to know was, *How are we to deal with the trauma?* Trauma, I would come to learn, while in the company of grief and loss, is not the same thing at all.

As the evening turned into night, everyone headed home, and eventually it was just our family and Thom and Dawn. We made up beds for the children. There was room for all of us downstairs in the beautiful walkout basement overlooking the lake. Christopher slept on a sofa in the living room and was thrilled that *his* bedroom had a widescreen TV. The girls were on the futon in Thom's study, happy to be together. Paul and I prayed with all three and tucked them in.

I got online to email a few people I wanted to make sure heard the news. My inbox was packed. One email was from the mother of one of Eden's classmates. The subject line read, "Ready and waiting to assist." When I read that, a part of my chest I didn't even know was constricted began to relax. I would later find out this same woman left a note in our mailbox, called my cell phone, and messaged me on Facebook, but it was the email that reached me first.

> Hi, guys. I don't even know what to say other than we are grateful the fire didn't claim your family. I know you're still processing and mourning right now, so let me be your thinking brain beyond, "What do we do today?" I already have a small group coming over here tomorrow a.m. to strategize immediate, mid-term, and long-term help/donations.

It was so strange to think that a group of people was meeting solely for the purpose of figuring out how to help my family. And this was only the beginning of what would become an extraordinary outpouring of kindness and generosity.

"Where have you been all my life?" I wrote back, only half joking.

Between email and Facebook, there were so many messages of concern, expressions of gratitude for our safety, promises of prayer, and offers of support. It was wonderfully overwhelming. I wanted to reply to each one, but a wave of exhaustion swept over me. I posted an update on Facebook:

> **deliverance: 1. an act or instance of delivering;**
> **2. salvation; 3. liberation**
>
> Today our home was destroyed by fire. The children are grieving and shaken, but Paul and I are so grateful for family, friends, and strangers who have come to our aid. We have lost "everything" but feel rich and free.

I climbed into bed next to Paul, who was already asleep. I looked up into the darkness. Everything had changed. Who could believe it? I thought of the children—safe and so close—of Jack at the foot of our bed, and Paul there beside me. Everything had changed, and anything that mattered remained.

five

The Beginning of Adjustment

Paul was just seventeen years old when his father died. It was a suicide after business struggles. The very next day, Paul had to help choose his grave. Walking around the cemetery felt like torture—all he wanted to do was be home in bed, curled in a ball. He vowed that if he ever became a father, he would never put his children in this position; he would take care of *everything* ahead of time.

When I was seventeen, my father discovered his bookkeeper had embezzled hundreds of thousands of dollars from the family business. Two years later, he and my mother sold our home to avoid bankruptcy. My older brother and I quit college to get jobs to help out, and it worked. They never went bankrupt, but something fundamental shifted in our family, and in more ways than one, my parents never fully recovered. For my siblings and me, losing our childhood home, a sprawling house set in a clearing of the most beautiful woods, felt like being kicked out of Eden.

When Paul and I became parents, all our financial decisions were made with security and stability in mind. We lived below our means by always paying cash for used cars and buying a house we could easily afford, which was tens of thousands of dollars less than what the bank was willing to lend us. We slowly redid the house, room by room. My love for good design sometimes clashed with my inherent frugality, but it was worth it to be patient. Our children would never know the stress and pain of losing their childhood home.

We had tried so hard to create a haven for our children, a place where they could be safe and protected. And now it was nothing but ash.

Of course, we were well insured. Two days after the fire, we had our first meeting with the adjuster, the person who assesses a claim and doles out the money on behalf of the insurance company. Our meeting was at 9:00 a.m.

"I want to get there a little early," Paul told me the night before. He was ready to go to the mat.

I woke up at 4:00 a.m. but still struggled to get out the door on time. My first problem was that I couldn't find any underwear. I ran the numbers: There was the pair I wore out of the fire and the three-pack Torey picked up for me at Target Sunday morning—it was only Tuesday, so I knew I had at least one pair left. There was only a small dresser in the room. Clothes with other donations had started pouring in, and Paul and I stacked our belongings on the floor around the perimeter of the room. Forty-eight hours into being dispossessed, and we were already beginning to feel overwhelmed by stuff.

I surveyed the tiny pile of donated clothes—*my new wardrobe*, it dawned on me. Finally I decided on an A-line white eyelet skirt that would have been lovely if it hadn't given me the silhouette of the Liberty Bell. The shirt I chose was a simple T. I liked the color, a pretty greenish-blue, but it was too small and strained across my chest, just as did the borrowed bra I had pressed into a service it was struggling to fulfill. I was a picture—a Glamour Not—but still.

I had no idea how long our appointment would be and knew it would be smart to pack a light lunch.

"Take whatever you want," Dawn said and gave me a canvas tote bag with the FedEx logo. I decided it could also serve as my quasi-purse.

Standing in the pantry with its floor-to-ceiling shelves stuffed with food, small appliances, and paper supplies, I just yawned and stared. *What was I doing again? Oh yeah. Lunch. Pack.*

I felt like I was walking underwater, moving slowly, pushing against a great resistance, but I finally gathered some food and filled water bottles for both Paul and me.

He had been pacing around the living room, ready to walk out the door for some time. In one hand he held his leather binder filled with notes, and in the other he clutched an insulated coffee cup—the kind with a handle that required him to make a fist and caused his elbow to jut out awkwardly. Normally he's a clean-cut, fresh-looking guy, but he was wearing what were now his only pair of pants—the shorts he pulled on when he jumped out of bed the morning of the fire and had worn for two days already. They were ash-stained and rumpled. His shirt was donated and wasn't quite long enough, so he tucked it into his dirty shorts, which seemed to be pulled up higher than usual.

"All set?" he asked in the carefully controlled, upbeat tone he employs when he's trying to keep his temper.

"Oh, I need to get coffee!" I had been up since four but somehow hadn't managed to pour a cup—a certain cry for help.

Paul sighed. "I'll wait for you in the truck."

A friend from Paul's office had, very generously, offered us the use of his enormous and brand-new pickup, which was an electric blue. To get in it, I had to hand the water bottle, coffee cup, and my tote bag to Paul and then use both hands to haul myself up and in.

We drove in silence. I knew Paul was annoyed with me for taking so long. I was certainly crabby with him for being oblivious to the fact that I had taken the time to pack something to eat for both of us. I thought he should be a bit more grateful. Even the most loving marriages can have well-worn ruts of familiar resentments. We sat strangely erect in our stained and ill-fitting clothes, looking like hillbillies who hit the jackpot. I felt foreign and uneasy. I was nervous about meeting with the adjuster.

Paul was ready to go. He stayed up late the night before reading an e-book about the insurance industry sent to him by a cousin of Thom's—a former insurance adjuster. His binder full of notes rested on the seat beside him. He projected confidence and strength and had the air of a person who had it all together.

But I thought he looked like an uptight hobo and felt the deep loathing that can sometimes coexist with profound love. I could feel my chest tightening. I stretched across the wide seat and reached for his hand.

"We need Jesus," I said, "because I hate you."

He couldn't disagree. I prayed as simply as I could for help, and for love and peace. When I finished, I didn't let go but continued to clutch his hand in both of mine. I remembered what the therapist had said about the children, how they would be an exaggerated form of their normal selves.

Paul had always been the wind beneath our organizational wings. Now he was dotting the thought of an "i" and crossing the suggestion of a "t," and I was literally wandering in circles and struggling to get dressed. This was an exaggerated and terrible form of who we were every single day.

Oh, the humanity.

In spite of all my delays, we still arrived fifteen minutes early. We parked in the driveway behind our burned-out cars and walked over to the deck. Soon after, the adjuster called to say he was half an hour away. This did not work for us. I shifted from nervousness to outrage that we had hurried, only to have to cool our heels next to the ruins of our home. We had managed—while emotionally and mentally rattled—to get up, scavenge our meager possessions, and get out to make it to our appointment *early*. My default is crabby judgment, while Paul is generally more easygoing, but this ticked him off too.

I would come to learn that every time I crossed onto the property, an internal timer would begin to tick. For a while, I would be able to walk around calmly, doing whatever I needed to do, even picking through the ruins of the house, until time abruptly, and entirely, ran out. My energy would fail and tears would start, and I'd know it was time to go. I didn't know this yet, but I already resented having to be there even a minute longer than absolutely necessary.

We walked past the burned-out house and back to the deck adjacent to the pool, and Paul pulled three chairs around one of the wrought-iron tables—two he positioned facing the west, and one on the other side facing the east and the sun just rising over the trees.

Normally we would give our guest the favorable spot, but we weren't entertaining.

"This is a negotiation," Paul said.

Finally the adjuster, a pudgy and balding man named Bob, arrived. He introduced himself in a blur of smiles, nonstop small talk, and vigorous handshaking.

"So sorry I'm late. I ran into traffic on 96, and it slowed me down." Paul and I both just looked at him. We weren't going to give him an inch, but he didn't seem to notice. He looked around at what remained of our home.

"Whew! This is going to be a total loss. And just between you and me, you're better off than if it was a partial claim. You get to start over with a clean slate." He looked again and shook his head. "I have a feeling I'm going to be writing for limits on this one."

Paul and I had looked over our policy the night before. We knew our coverage, the exact dollar amount. I imagined Bob writing us a big fat check that very day. *Whoopee! Thank you!* But he didn't pull out his checkbook. We moved back to the deck. Paul showed Bob to his seat, and we all sat down.

"It's going to get up there today!" he said. After the obligatory minute's chat about the weather, his demeanor changed completely and abruptly. He looked down, his face grave. "Before we start, I just want to say how sorry I am for your tragedy. A house fire is a terrible, terrible experience, and I'm very sorry you're going through this."

We accepted his condolences, and he shifted again just as quickly and completely. His face brightened. It was clear he had checked off "Extend rote condolences" from the list and was ready to move on to the next order of business.

I pulled my notebook out of my bag, the one my friend had given me the morning of the fire, two days and a lifetime ago. I opened it and set it on the table in front of me, clicked my pen, and sat up straight. Paul's binder was already open, his pen cocked and loaded over a clean legal pad. We were ready.

But no, Bob started to tell us a long and rambling story about trying to buy tickets to a football game for his college-age son. Although many of us love to tell them, I don't know anyone who wants to listen to a boring and seemingly pointless story. Sitting there, I had the same feeling I had the morning of the fire—that intense anxiety I felt waiting to cross the road when the car lights flashed in the darkness. I just wanted to get to the policy. I just wanted to face facts. I wanted to move on and deal.

". . . and then Bobby said, 'Dad, you're *always* late!'" Bob laughed.

Paul and I exchanged a quick glance. Clearly, Bob had forgotten the excuses about traffic he made less than an hour before and was oblivious that he had given himself away. He abruptly shifted again, opened his briefcase, and explained the basics of our policy.

With the loss of a home, the claim is broken down into two categories:

structure and contents. The structure is the house itself—the roof and walls—and its value is determined by its size and the quality of construction. Bob explained the maximum amount we were insured for. Not how much we were insured for, but the maximum amount. I noticed the distinction, although I wasn't quite sure what it meant.

Contents are everything in the structure: furniture, books and art, pots and pans, plates and cutlery, toys, toiletries, and technology. Everything down to the box of paper clips in my burned-out desk had a value and would need to be listed and appraised.

"Something I'm going to do for you is bring in content specialists. I know a great company. I work with them all the time—and they'll go through everything that's left and create an inventory, which is a list of everything they can identify. Some companies would make you prepare the inventory yourself, but we want to help you all we can."

"What about all the things that burned?" I asked. More than half our house was ash.

"For that, you will need to make your own inventory. Go room by room—if you have any pictures, that will help a lot—just write down everything you can think of. Everything has value. Tweezers, nail polish, even a bag of cotton balls! But you should know, you're going to forget things. Sometime in the future, long after everything is settled, you'll remember something, and you're going to kick yourself. But don't worry about it. It happens. Everyone forgets things." I thought it was easy for him to be blasé about other people's losses.

Then it was back to another long and rambling story about his wife, who was taking a pottery class taught by nuns.

I stopped listening until he abruptly shifted to—

"Outdoor structures! I can see you are a gardener, and the maximum allowance—"

A car pulled into the driveway, and a small man got out.

"Over here, Stan!" Bob called out.

We all stood to greet him.

"This is Stan. He's our investigator. He'll be taking a look around."

We all shook hands. Stan's face was stern, uncompromising. I knew we were under suspicion. Again. He asked us a few questions like the ones the detectives asked: if we had any enemies, how our finances were, any changes in employment. He was abrupt, almost curt. He didn't even offer pretend condolences, like Bob had.

And then, there was an imperceptible shift, and I knew we were no longer under suspicion. His whole demeanor changed, and he was friendly and talkative.

Bob motioned us back, and we left Stan to his investigation.

We spent several more hours with Bob, going over our policy line by line. There weren't really any surprises, until we learned our cars wouldn't be covered. That claim would go through our auto insurance. Since we had paid cash for both and they were older vehicles, we only held collision coverage. We had planned to replace Paul's elderly Camry that year, but it was still running fine, and he had decided to see how long it would last. We had the money saved to replace it, but losing both cars overnight was a serious and unexpected expense. We had an emergency fund, but when I began to mentally deduct two cars, basic clothing, and supplies, my mind raced.

With every category, Bob told us what we were covered up to. "Up to." I had known this would be a negotiation and began to understand why. Homeowners can buy as much coverage as they want, but when it comes time to make a claim, the onus is on them to prove their lost property was actually worth that amount. The settlement is uncertain, and determining what it will be is called "the adjustment." It's funny, when you think of something being adjusted, the inference is that it's being improved—that the after is always better than the before. But anyone who's been through any sort of crisis can tell you that's not always the case.

When you need to adjust to a new situation, the sense is it's the acceptance of something *different*, and not necessarily better. We were certainly adjusting to so much, even to the adjustment itself, and I could only hope we would come through it better off.

Bob droned on, every few categories interrupted by a long and pointless story obviously told to engender rapport and trust. With each one, my loathing increased, but Bob remained oblivious to the fact that he was repelling the ones he hoped to attract.

Finally the policy was exhausted. Bob looked up. "You need to know what you are about to go through is incredibly stressful. Right now, you're still in shock, but in about two to three weeks, after the shock has worn off, it's going to hit you. I always tell my clients to get away for a weekend. You're going to need a break."

I robotically wrote down "2–3 weeks" in my notebook. This didn't sound good, but at least it was something I could count on.

"I need to warn you about another thing," Bob said. "There are going to be ambulance chasers coming out of the woodwork, trying to get you to sign with them, telling you they want to help you and that they'll get you so much more money, but going with them would be a mistake. I'm here for you. Just give me a chance. Let Uncle Bob take care of you. There's only so much money, and why would you want to give a bunch of it to some other guys when you can work with me directly and keep it all. Worst-case scenario, you're not satisfied, you can take us to court—and who do you think the judge and jury are going to side with? You poor homeowners, or the big, bad insurance company?" He nodded his head as if to confirm his own statement.

I knew the information Paul had read to prepare for this meeting was written by a public adjuster—or "ambulance chaser," according to Bob. Paul told me they are a liaison between the homeowner and the insurance company. They represent and negotiate on the homeowner's behalf. We could do it ourselves, but the way Paul looked at it, it would be like hiring a realtor, and the premium we paid—in this case, a percentage of the insurance settlement—would be more than worth it. The night before, that made perfect sense to me too. But sitting here across from Bob, I wasn't so sure. The thought of others pushing and pulling at us, trying to persuade us to sign with them made me anxious. And there was only so much money to be had. Why would we want to give away a percentage right off the top? Bob seemed like a goofball, but maybe we *should* give him a chance. I looked at Paul, but he was looking straight ahead, his jaw set.

Bob snapped his binder shut. "Well, that's everything. Stan wants to take you through the house to check for any valuables that may have survived. I'll check back in a couple days."

We found Stan raking through the layers of wreckage in the garage.

"You're sure you set the gas can here?" he asked Paul.

"Absolutely sure. I mowed that afternoon and rolled the mower here." Paul pointed to the area where his garage stall had been. I had been right there to see him do it, so I knew it was true.

"I can't find it."

I looked at the total devastation that had been our garage. The obvious answer was it had melted into nothing. Stan read my mind.

"When they melt down, they form a disc." He held his hands out to show something the size of a bread plate. He looked back at the garage. "That's what I've been looking for."

I wasn't sure what this meant. Was this news good for our status on the suspect list, or bad?

"It's a funny thing—oftentimes the arsonist will take the can with him."

So it's good! I exhaled.

Stan led us through the house to look for any valuables. I didn't want anything. We had already gone back on the night of the fire and pulled out the few paintings and any official papers that survived. I didn't really care about anything else. I didn't want to be bogged down with stuff, and I didn't want to be painfully reminded of the things I had already lost. I took my little bit of jewelry and was good. I didn't want to be in the house. It was painful and strange wandering through the ruins of my own life.

I asked Stan what he thought about the children coming back to the house. Christopher had been bugging us about going through his room and trying to salvage some of his belongings.

"My inclination has been to keep them away, but the therapist I spoke with said we could leave it up to them."

"With all due respect," Stan began with a tone that held no respect, "she doesn't know what she's talking about. I go into these houses all the time. It's devastating for adults. For kids, their home is their safe place. Their rooms are their world. You don't want to let your kids see that destroyed. How old are they?"

I told him.

"If it was me, I definitely wouldn't let your youngest near the place. Your son obviously wants to come, and he's older. I guess it depends with your older girl, but the youngest? If it was me, I wouldn't let her see it."

By then, it was late in the afternoon. I called my mother, who soon brought Christopher by, and Stan took him to his room. He grabbed a lot of things, including several waterlogged books. Some were treasures, and one he had been reading the night before the fire. He was most happy to find the Swiss Army knife my mother had given him just that Christmas.

"Does it feel better having some of your things?" I asked.

He nodded, and his smile lit up his face. "What if I went to the girls' room and tried to get some things for them?"

Stan offered to help Christopher look through the girls' room. He was obviously impressed by Christopher's thoughtfulness.

Meanwhile, Paul needed to look for his computer from work. The IT department wanted to see if they could salvage the hard drive.

Paul remembered tucking it under the bed before he went to sleep that last night. Our bedroom was in the part of the house that was somewhat intact. We had to walk past my study to get to it. The ceiling had collapsed, and our bed was piled with drywall and insulation. Paul borrowed Stan's rake and tried to reach under the bed with it.

Our bedroom wasn't large even before the ceiling fell in, so there wasn't much room to move. I stood outside and talked to Paul through a window. I was standing in the demolished garden bed where the year before I had transplanted ostrich ferns under a weeping cherry on the corner. Every morning I had looked out and counted ferns that, even in late June, were still emerging. They were all gone now. Only the trunk on the cherry tree remained. I peered into our bedroom. Our clothes, smoke-stained and soaked, hung in the closet. The books Paul and I were reading that last night were on our respective nightstands. It was a terrible still life, a portrait of our once domestic lives now in ruins—preserved but destroyed.

Paul bent low and reached as far as he could under the bed, gently raking the debris.

I thought of the blaring alarms, running out of the room, smacking

Christopher's leg, running into the night, the flames reaching into the treetops. A wave of exhaustion lifted and fell.

I rested my forehead on the window frame.

"How do people do it?"

Paul looked up. "What do you mean?"

"We all got out. How do people who have lost someone in a fire manage a claim?"

"I'm guessing most of them don't. They probably take whatever's offered and quickly settle."

"I don't know how I would face this without you." I wanted to reach through the window to touch him but held back, leery of the broken and jagged glass.

"I don't know how I would face this without *you*."

We were silent for a moment.

"I don't want to white-knuckle things," I said.

"What do you mean?"

"I mean I don't want to make things any more or less than they are. I don't want to be brave and fake it till we make it for the sake of Jesus."

Paul smiled. "We'll let it be what it is."

We just looked at each other for a moment. In the ebb and flow of daily life, how rarely we truly see one another. I looked at this man, whom I had known and loved since I was a girl and he was a boy. I thought of our marriage, which had already weathered so much, and I knew, in some ways, that this was just another fire we would make it through—we *were* making it through. There would almost certainly be more days when one or the other of us would be our worst self. But I also knew, as we stretched and bent in the midst of this stressful and difficult time, that Paul and I could also be extraordinary forms of who we always had been and still were.

six

Our (First) Puppy Wish List

Anyone who has lost a loved one can tell you that grief is not a linear journey. My father died seven years before our house burned down, but the stress and pain opened up a fresh sorrow. I so wanted my dad. One Sunday, a few weeks after the fire, I thought of him while we were singing in church and began to weep. Eden, who was standing beside me, turned and buried her face in my side, and I could feel her shaking. I sat down and put my arm around her. Tears were streaming down her face too.

I leaned in. "What's going on?"

"I miss Grandpa!" she cried out, sobbing.

"Me too," I said. "I do too." It astonished me how exactly her emotions mirrored my own. *We need to mourn*, I thought.

Before my dad died, I had never really mourned anything. It's not that I hadn't lost other loved ones or been through hard times; I just hadn't mourned them. During Christopher's prolonged diagnosis, I didn't know how to hold my pain and still hold my faith. I didn't think I was angry—I couldn't be—because Christopher was a gift from God, and to be angry would be rejecting my boy. Or that's what I made up. I talked about faith and peace that I didn't fully possess. I didn't know how to stand in the paradox of trust and sorrow, of faith and grief, of love and disappointment. I didn't know how to mourn.

After my dad died at the age of sixty-four—nowhere near "full of years," as the Bible calls a long life—the overwhelming emotion I felt was anger. I was so mad at him for not taking better care of himself. I was angry we had both wasted so much time. My heart ached that my opportunity to be his daughter was over and, since Paul's dad was long dead, that my kids wouldn't have a grandfather. There was nothing in me I could summon to even try to make it OK. I was utterly bereft, empty of everything except grief and rage.

When Jesus taught his followers, he often used analogies to explain profound things. But there were times he was completely direct. In his most famous sermon—the Sermon on the Mount—he said, among other things, "Blessed are those who mourn, for they will be comforted." He was making a promise without qualifications. In the early days after my dad's death, it seemed impossible. I couldn't quite believe it, but what else could I do. *Prove it*, I thought, not knowing that was a prayer.

How do you mourn? I didn't know. All day, every day, my mind raced. I thought about what my father should have done differently, what I should have done differently. I was filled with regret. I hated our ending. I so wished we'd had a different story.

I had committed to mourn this, but I didn't really know exactly what that meant. I knew how to minimize things and then be bitter, but I'd never purely mourned a single thing.

So I prayed in a way that was a lot of talking out loud. "I'm so sad Dad is dead. I'm angry he didn't take better care of himself. I wish my children had a grandfather. I'm mad he gave up." On and on and on.

One day as I was crying and grieving, the thought came to me that my father had it all figured out. He was seeing through a glass clearly. Now that he had died, he knew how to live. I felt compelled to pray for his perspective and was astonished at how quickly my prayer was answered. Almost immediately, I felt detached from material things. I really noticed it when I glanced at a box of family pictures. Normally I would have felt a pang of guilt that they weren't in a scrapbook, but I felt nothing. I was the mother of young children. The absence of guilt in conjunction with pictures of my kids was practically a miracle. I felt clarity about what was important and what could fall to the side. I didn't feel as burdened by my home. With my dad, I was able to move through the anger and work through the grief, and, eventually, I felt peace. I was comforted. Learning to mourn changed everything for me.

In the early days after the fire, I knew we would need to mourn it, and I was so relieved I could just let things be what they were, as Paul had said. Of course, I had no idea how hard they were going to be.

The next Sunday after Eden and I had both wept in church, she began to cry again during the singing. I bent down. "Grandpa?"

She shook her head.

"What is it?"

"Jack," she whispered.

What was the problem with our dog? "What about Jack?"

"He's going to die someday!" This was said in a sob that seemed to be ripped out of her. I sat down and pulled her onto my lap. She shoved her face against my neck and wet it with her tears. I petted her hair. A lump bloomed in my throat. Even if I was capable of speech, what could I say? Jack *was* going to die someday.

Eden was five months old when my father died. Although she has no memory of him, she has grown up "missing" him. How often isn't the thing we've never had the thing we long for most keenly?

We marked my father's death with her life. *How long has Dad been gone? How old is Eden?* From birth, she understood mortality just by his absence. I knew the only reason she was crying about Jack today was that someone had set our house on fire. I had known she would one day understand that none of us escape death, even her beloved dog, but I also knew the only reason she was crying about it this day was that she was beginning to process her unfathomable loss. I hated that her normal and childlike illusion of invincibility, that swaddling veil of security, had been ripped away prematurely—here was yet another layer of the fire's sorrows to mourn. I clutched her to me, and resting my cheek on her head, I gently rocked. The singing wove over and around us as we cried together.

Jack was the one member of our family who was handling life after the fire without a hitch. When we arrived at Dawn and Thom's, he happily joined the fray with his three dog "cousins"—a Weimaraner, a German shorthaired pointer, and a Goldendoodle. The four big dogs played together and roughhoused all day long. Jack was living the dream, and it was nice to see at least one of us thriving.

Up until we got Jack, I wasn't really a dog person. With a few exceptions, I experienced dogs as panting messes of fur, drool, and naughty behavior. But then I gave birth to Christopher, an animal lover with a passion for dogs in particular. As soon as he was ambulatory, he was hitting on strange dogs wherever he could—parks, garage sales, the sidewalk in front of our house (dog owners in a hurry learned to avoid our street), anywhere really.

When Christopher was not quite two years old, we stopped at a yard sale where the homeowner's friendly dog was lounging in the driveway. I remember it was a smaller breed, because Christopher had to bend over to pet, pet, pet in the calm and gentle way I taught him. The owner, an older lady, asked if we had a dog of our own, and I told her we did not.

She fixed me with a gimlet eye. "You have *got* to get this child a dog." She didn't come right out and accuse me of neglect, but it was implied. Her intensity made me nervous, and yet I knew she was right; something deep inside of Christopher lit up and came alive only when he was with a dog.

The thing is, not long after Christopher's first birthday, we had learned he was deaf—and that was just the beginning. We were still in the middle of a mass of testing and diagnoses for him, and I was extra busy having a difficult pregnancy with Lydia. I ran the numbers—toddler with special needs + newborn + puppy/dog = *insanity*. Although Paul had grown up with dogs and loved them, he agreed entirely. The prudent thing for our little family was to wait, which we did—for another nine years.

Anyone whose dog I admired said the same thing: "In the beginning, it's a lot like having another child." I had two and then three children of my own, so I knew that was code for "crapload of work," and this was not encouraging. But there was my boy, with a multiplicity of special needs and a *passion* for dogs.

So I did what I always do in times of uncertainty: I read. I plowed through book after book—from training and behavioral guides to personal essays and memoirs—anything I could get my hands on about life with a dog. I came across something the writer Jon Katz said in one of his books: At the end of the day, a dog is an animal, and even a good dog, a well-trained dog, will do stupid and disgusting things. He gave the example of his Lab, who loved to roam in the woods, find vile things to eat, and then be sick inside the house. Most people don't want a real animal, Katz contends; they want a Disney dog. When I read that, I realized a Disney dog was exactly what I wanted, and up until that moment, I had thought if I worked hard enough, I could transform an animal into a cartoon fantasy. I faced reality with equal parts relief and disappointment.

As years passed, Paul's opposition to adding any kind of dog to our chaotic household did not. So I didn't try to wheedle or cajole. Frankly, I wasn't entirely sure it *was* a good idea. Maybe we couldn't handle training and taking care of a dog. Maybe it would be a mistake.

One day, in one of my many dog books, I read a story about a little boy who had trouble making friends. His parents bought him a German shepherd, and it became the boy's best friend and constant companion. I thought what a comfort an animal can be for a child, a safe haven so vital, even in a good and loving home. I thought of my boy, who, with his various disabilities, wasn't like "all the other kids," and I wanted him to have a friend who would always be there, in every sense. I showed this story to Paul. "Would you be willing to pray about it?" I asked. He said he would pray every day for six weeks. I prayed too for a week or so and then forgot about it.

One day Paul said, "OK."

"What?"

"I said, 'OK.' I'm ready to get a dog."

I was excited and a little scared, but we told the kids, who were thrilled.

"What kind of dog do we want?" I asked when we gathered for a little family meeting. They began to list attributes they were hoping to find in our dog: kind, sweet, goofy, smart enough to train, obedient, loving, handsome. I wrote them all down and taped the list to the front of one of the kitchen cabinets.

"Let's pray for our puppy while we wait," I said. Almost every night, at least one of them remembered to pray. It was early spring, so we weren't in a hurry, but I began to look. Because neither Paul nor I had ever trained a dog and our children were younger, I focused on breeds that were highly trainable, easygoing, and affectionate and fell in love with English Labradors. Unfortunately, their price was so prohibitive I set that possibility aside. Petfinder became my daily haunt for weeks, but there was a strange dearth of puppies.

A few days before Easter, I was reading the paper and happened to turn to the classifieds. Right at the top was a small ad: Black Labrador Puppy, 12 weeks, stockier breed. I wondered if this could possibly be an English Lab. The price listed was less than half—more like a third—of what I had seen in other places. I scrabbled for the phone.

The breeder was an older woman. She and her husband had been running a kennel and breeding Labradors for years.

"Now our pups are shorter and thicker than other Labradors."

"Are they English?" I asked.

They were!

"Normally I get more than double what I'm asking, but he's the last of the litter, and I just want to find him a good home."

I wanted the chance to be a good home—especially for a third of the usual price! We arranged a visit. They were about an hour south of us, but, serendipitously, Paul and I were already planning later that week to take the kids to a science museum that was minutes from the kennel.

The breeder and her husband were a kindly older couple. First they introduced the mother of the litter, a beautiful, big black Labrador. She was enormous and sweet, a real beauty. We all sat on the floor, and the breeder brought in the puppy to a collective "Aw!" He was a chubby little black with two coals for eyes. Paul and I let the kids take turns holding him. He was excited and nibbling on the girls' hair. He was adorable.

After a bit, we went out for lunch to talk about it.

"What do you think?" I asked the kids on the way to the restaurant. "Do you think he's our puppy?" For Christopher and Eden, there was no doubt, but Lydia, who was only nine at the time but wise beyond her years, hesitated.

"Maybe we should think about it. Maybe this isn't the best time for us to get a puppy. Maybe we aren't ready. A dog is a big responsibility." Boy howdy.

"How about we pray and then give it a little time while we eat, and we can talk about it afterward." Before lunch, we prayed for the puppy and asked God to show us if he was the right dog for our family.

Back in the van, we talked it over, and everyone agreed this was the puppy for us.

We returned to the breeder's house, and as I was writing the check, the puppy waddled over and slumped against me. I felt his warm bulk, and tenderness overcame me.

"Now you know he has an overbite, right?" the breeder asked.

"Excuse me?"

"He has an overbite."

Since she hadn't said anything before, it was the first I had heard about this, and as the mother of two children with underbites—one so profound she had begun her orthodontic journey at the age of four—I was keenly interested.

"Is that a problem?"

"If the teeth grow too long, they may need to be filed down."

Dogs need dental work? I looked down at the furry little blob resting against me and felt his warmth and the weight of his plumpness. The check was half written. What was I going to do? We had talked and prayed . . . I finished writing the check.

Jack was twelve weeks old when we brought him home on Good Friday. It took us several days to name him. Paul and I had never named with a committee before, and several factions emerged. We came up with a long list of possibilities, but none of us agreed on any one of them. Eden and I were pulling for Scout—with Christopher's support—while Lydia was lobbying hard for Isaac. We considered Huckleberry because he just seemed like a Huckleberry-ish sort of dog, but I knew we would call him "Huck" and decided it probably wasn't a good idea to name him something that rhymed with—well, we decided against it. It was when Paul started pushing Buckley that I panicked.

"How about Blackjack?" I asked, "And we can call him Jack for short."

I thought of the Little House on the Prairie books, which I had loved as a little girl, and of Laura's beloved bulldog—her "good dog Jack." That sounded just right. Everyone, after a little persuading of Lydia, agreed. Jack it was.

He was a sweet and relatively docile pup, but nothing can really prepare you for the relentlessness of the early days of puppy ownership—and a Labrador retriever puppy at that. I had sleep-trained three human babies with less stress than crate-training this pup. One of our many books recommended having the kennel in one's room, so that's what we did. Which made his heart-piercing cries all the more audible in the wee hours.

One of my aunts had a specific spot in her yard where her dog did his toileting, and I aimed to train Jack to do the same. A steep hill rose just beyond our back deck, and about halfway up was the perfect spot. It was within our fence but far enough away to be hidden from view. This required me, every time the dog had to go out, to lead/carry him to his spot and set him right where I wanted him and then command, "Do it, Jack! Do it! Here's your spot; do it!" The second he did any sort of business, I exploded in encouragement and praise to help him make the connection. I had insisted on waiting until spring because I didn't want to trudge halfway up a snow-covered hill. But a late blizzard hit the night we got Jack, and that's exactly what I did the first week we had him.

When he woke up in the middle of the night, I took him up the hill. In the beginning, the snow was so deep that I had to carry him. Once I got him there, he was content to just sniff around and then sit and blink at me. Later, when the snow melted, he'd nibble leaves while I shone a high-powered flashlight at him to keep an eye on whether or not he did any business in order to immediately praise him.

I worried he was eating ivy, which I Googled later and found out was poisonous, and then another night, I accidentally shone the flashlight right in his face and worried I had blinded him.

Then, of course, he had a fun little trick of peeing on the kitchen floor within minutes of coming back inside.

Still, he was fat and happy and adorable, but not ten days after we brought him home, the vet informed us he was on the brink of obesity. Apparently I had been feeding him twice as much as necessary. The owner of two Labs herself, she recommended I replace his food bowl with something called a Food Cube—a plastic box that would require him to push and turn it over to dispense the food three or four kibbles at a time. She thought it was about twenty-five dollars. I mentally put this at the bottom of my "To Buy" list, since that month's budget was straining from the hundreds of dollars I had already spent on a crate and two gates, brushes and shampoos, a collar and tags, toys and a leash, examinations and vaccinations, pounds and pounds of food, and the now-deficient bowls—not to mention the overbite dog himself.

Two weeks later, we were back for more shots. Jack loved going to the vet. He loved most everything, especially if it involved other dogs. As soon as I opened the van door, he was straining and pulling to get inside the office. We were working on his manners, so I made him wait while I entered first. This took time, energy, and strength. It was like having a very small and demented bull on a leash. With the kids, it was always a circus—monitoring them, controlling Jack, and answering any questions the staff had. I usually left the office with a headache and in a sweat. And this was a routine visit!

A month or so later, I called the vet because Jack had kept me up most of the night with jags of coughing that should have brought up major organs. He was still his chipper self, but they told me to bring him in immediately for examination.

He didn't have any blockage, and after a thorough examination, the doctor suspected he had inhaled a kibble. It worked its way out, but his trachea was irritated, causing him to cough.

With a little medication, his inflamed throat soon healed, but for that and the examination and the sedation, the financial damage was $113.26—$88.26 of which I recognized was Stupid Tax for not buying the stinking Food Cube immediately after the vet recommended it. And yet I was happy to pay, having spent the night imagining what Jack might have swallowed (a stuffed animal, a large block, a long wool sock, an underwire bra, to name his favorite chews) and worrying that he needed extensive and expensive surgery . . . if he lived. I knew my children's grief would be tremendous when Jack died someday, but five weeks after we got him was unthinkable.

"What are we going to do with you, Jackie Boy?" I said when we were home and resting on the lawn outside. He just stared at me and then quietly bit off a pansy from a nearby flowerpot. I didn't think it was toxic, but swept it out of his mouth with my finger just to be safe.

Four days after his discharge, he was still coughing. I called the office.

"Hi, this is Alison Hodgson—"

"How's Jack?" the receptionist asked. In eleven years with the same pediatrician, the receptionist still couldn't match me with my kids. And my vet's office knew my dog and me by name in less than a month. Whether or not that was a good thing, I wasn't sure. Regardless, the coughing cleared up the next day.

On May 18, we were back in for his last round of shots, and I scheduled him to be neutered on June 22. *After that*, I thought, *he and my checkbook will be free for a year.*

On May 29, I called to ask about a cut on his mouth that had stopped bleeding, but I wondered if I needed to/if it was safe to apply Neosporin. They told me it was safe, but that he would only lick it off. Since the bleeding had stopped, he was probably OK, but they wanted me to keep an eye on his eating and drinking.

On June 9, a Saturday, Jack began limping for no apparent reason. There was no way I was going to call the office on the weekend. I decided to keep an eye on him and hoped he would get better.

The following Monday, June 11, he was still limping, and I reluctantly called. Since there was no known trauma, they told me to continue monitoring him and to try to limit his activity. I needed to call if things got worse or if he hadn't improved any by the end of the week.

The next morning, almost as soon as I saw him, I knew something was wrong. Jack was standing on the deck, licking the residue of vinegar and baking soda from the homemade rocket Christopher had set off the day before.

"Jack, no!" I shouted.

He looked up and blinked. Something about him looked off. Was it his head? Was it even possible that his head had . . . shrunk? I staggered back.

I cannot call the vet! was my first thought.

I took another look. Jack blinked at me placidly. He was fine. Despite this declaration and my resistance to call the vet, I kept an uneasy eye on him throughout the day. At one point, I even did a kind of examination— pressing his sides, feeling for his ribs.

My sister, Torey, called, and I told her the latest installment in the saga of Jack. "I'm sure he's fine, and I can't call the vet *again*. They probably think I have Munchausen by proxy—with a canine."

"What!"

"You know, that syndrome where parents pretend their kids are sick to get attention—Munchausen syndrome by proxy—except they're going to think I have it with Jack."

The kids and I were outside most of the day, and Jack was always right with us. I did notice he seemed to be panting a bit more than normal, and he was certainly drinking a lot of water, but I attributed it to the warmth of the day.

That is what they call denial.

When my husband, Paul, came home, there was the normal mayhem of kids running to greet him and the dog barking on the periphery. "Paul, take a look at Jackie Boy, would you?" I asked.

We both turned to look at the dog standing in the doorway. I gasped. His body looked twice its normal size, and his large, blockish head appeared even smaller than it had that morning. His expression was strained.

"That ain't right," Paul said.

"Do you think I should call the vet?"

"Um, yeah."

I ran to get the phone. A recording saying that the office was closed was the answer, but I waited to leave a message. "This is Alison Hodgson—"

The receptionist picked up the phone. "How's Jack?" she asked.

I told her.

She asked me a few questions and then put me on hold to check in with one of the doctors. A minute later, she was back.

"The doctor recommends you take him to the emergency clinic." She gave me the number. "I hope he's OK," she said with obvious concern.

Torey rushed over to stay with the kids, and Paul and I left with Jack.

At the clinic, they admitted him right away and took X-rays. A doctor met with us privately and attached one of the X-rays to the light box. Jack's spine was immediately recognizable, flowing across the top of the X-ray, and I could see it was a profile shot of his hindquarters, but that was about it. The doctor pointed to a large, oblong cottony mass. Had Jack scarfed down a bag of cotton balls? I didn't think we owned that many.

"What is that?" I asked.

"It appears to be kibble."

It looked like there were thousands of them.

I looked at Paul. "I don't know when he could have eaten all that." Paul shook his head. Neither of us knew. We'd been asked here, and by our doctor, if Jack could have gotten into his food, but I didn't think he had; it was stored in the laundry room, which was down a hall off the kitchen, and the door was always shut. Since Jack was always underfoot, my feet in particular, I couldn't think of a time he had been in the laundry room, but clearly he had.

The doctor laid out her plan. The first step was to induce vomiting. If that didn't work, the next step would be a gastric lavage, where Jack, under sedation, would have a tube slid down his esophagus into his stomach, and they would pump out the food.

"He's going to have his stomach pumped?" I asked, picturing a drugged-out rock star. It was so melodramatic—nothing I ever expected to be associated with my sweet puppy.

"Hopefully not, but yes, that's what gastric lavage is," the doctor said and then turned back to Jack.

Hopefully not indeed! Every step of Jack's care we were given an estimate of the cost of each proposed treatment. We knew that just getting him in the door, examined, and X-rayed got us up around $250 already. The less they did, the cheaper it was.

After more than an hour, the doctor returned with bad news: the vomit had not been induced. Our options were to go ahead with the gastric lavage or take Jack home and hope the food would pass normally. The risk in taking him home was that the food would harden and rupture his stomach, necessitating emergency surgery.

I leaned forward. "How much is the gastric lavage?"

The doctor repeated the financial range of the procedure.

"And what are we up to now with the induction?"

The doctor ballparked me on our tab and left us alone to talk.

I added the two and shook my head. "What do you think?" I asked Paul.

"I think we should do it. We're already in this far, and when we take Jack home, I want to know he's OK."

I thought of losing Jack and pictured Christopher. When he cried, tears seemed to shoot out of his eyes. There was no way we were taking that dog home until we could assure Christopher and the girls that he was all better.

Since Jack had been admitted, we could hear him barking almost nonstop in the back of the clinic, and I felt a new and strange pull of tenderness for that silly and troublesome dog. When his barking quieted, we knew the sedation had taken effect and the gastric lavage was underway. Although I had run an all-out offensive to get a puppy, it was only because I thought it would be good for the children. Paul, who had so heartily resisted, was the one—along with the kids, of course—who immediately fell in love. For me, Jack was constant work and worry. He was also adorable and sweet, but the former far outweighed the latter.

Time passed so slowly in that dismal waiting room, but finally, almost five hours after he had been admitted, Jack was ready to go home. He staggered out with his tail wagging. Paul and I both winced when he came close enough to smell his vile breath.

In the car I sat with him in the backseat. He lounged across my lap and stuck his nose out the window I had rolled down as far as it would go and sniffed the air. Paul looked back at us and smiled. "Jackie Boooooooy!" he crooned. Jack pulled his head back in and thumped his tail against the seat.

I wish I could say this was the last of Jack's mishaps and emergencies— the most dramatic and expensive, but *not*, alas, the last.

Who could know that he would have a strange reaction to the anesthesia when he was neutered (June 22), making him hyper and frantic instead of sleepy as expected, and that he would bash his large cone into everything, particularly my shins, for the better part of a week? Or that he would leap onto the counter and eat an unknown amount of chocolate chips (June 26)? He would fall off our deck (July 16) and develop another limp, requiring X-rays and medication? He would make another dash for the laundry room (August 9) and scarf down a day's worth of food before I dragged him away? His limp would return again (August 22) and again (December 27)? He would swallow a rubber yo-yo (April 9 the following spring), necessitating another induction of vomit, and this time the vomit would be induced?

But also who could know that Paul and I would begin to get up early every morning to walk Jack for his sake and find that it was for our good too, in so many ways? All of us would laugh and play as a family even more. And somewhere in the midst of those visits and calls, month after month in the day-to-day keeping of that dog, I would begin to deeply care for him rather than simply take care of him.

After that first tumultuous year, Jack settled down, and our only visits to the vet were for his annual checkup. As the years passed, he became almost everything we had hoped he would be and fulfilled almost every one of our wishes on the long-forgotten list, still taped to the cupboard door on the morning our house was set on fire.

seven

It Only Takes One Fat Pug to Get an Obsession Going

Not quite a year before our fire, and after almost seventeen years of marriage, I fell in love with a guy I met online. He was short and kinda stout—the less charitable might have called him fat—and he wasn't handsome in the traditional sense, but there was just something about him. It was love at first sight.

As you can imagine, Paul was less than thrilled. "The heart wants what it wants," I told him, and my heart wanted a fat pug named Tonka.

Somehow I had caught the pug bug. And before I knew it, I found myself browsing on a very dangerous website—Petfinder.com.

It all began innocently enough.

First, there was a plump little fawn pug named Beijing we met at a furniture consignment shop I liked to visit. The shop was constantly getting new pieces in, and as soon as some pieces came in the door, they sold, so I had made it a habit to stop by every few weeks to check out new arrivals. I almost always had my kids in tow. One of the first times we went, we were excited to see that the salesperson had brought in his dog—a pug named Beijing—who ran out to greet customers. The first time we visited, it was a quiet day, and as soon as her owner saw our obvious enthusiasm, he showed us all of Beijing's tricks. Her most impressive one was when she would spin around in a circle on command. With her fat little body, this was especially funny. She always landed in the sitting position, with a look of excited expectance. She always seemed so happy to show off.

Thinking about how exhausting it was to train Jack in the very basics, I was impressed. "How did you train her?"

"Oh, she knew these when we rescued her. She was completely trained and then taught so many tricks—she clearly came from a good home."

"Where did you find her?"

"There's a pug rescue here in town."

I didn't know anything about rescues. But this planted a seed: Rescued pugs could be fully trained and wonderful.

Not long after, a dear friend was talking about his brother and sister-in-law, who lived in the country with their menagerie of children and animals—hamsters, several cats, a golden retriever, and two pugs to top it all off.

At first, they only had one pug. When his sister-in-law was recovering after a miscarriage, the pug began sleeping on her chest. Her husband loved the dog too, so they got a second one for him. "There's nothing better than a napping pug," he told our friend Dan, which made me laugh. I pictured this loud and busy household finally quieting down at night, with the exhausted parents stretched out on sofas, pugs perched on their chests.

"How are pugs with children?" I asked. Beijing was so friendly with my three, but maybe she was the exception.

"Oh, they're great," Dan said. "They're wonderful."

Memories of Beijing, as well as the image of pugs snoozing on chests at the end of the day, were dancing in my head. I blame them for why I found myself casually checking out pugs on Petfinder about nine months before the fire.

It was almost immediate—BAM! There was Tonka, tongue out, with a wide-open mouth that seemed to smile, wearing a red bandana and leaping through the screen straight into my heart. Any good rescue knows that a variety of pictures is key on Petfinder, and there were three of Tonka. In every one of them, his tongue was stuck out and his winning personality shone. He had looks, personality, and a gorgeous bod—the total package. The written description was even better: "Tonka is housebroken and great with children!" He loved taking walks—not that he did any actual walking because he was so fat. The writer didn't flat-out say it, but anyone reading—and with eyes to see—could figure that out. His foster mother pushed him in a stroller, and he loved all the attention he got. He was working on getting in shape by actually walking a little every day.

I had always been careful to avoid feeding Jack table food because Labs are so prone to obesity, but the truth is, I love a fat dog. I knew it was wrong to fatten one up, but to rescue a portly fellow was another thing altogether.

Short story: I was hooked.

I immediately showed Tonka's pictures to Paul. He agreed he was cute and then pointed out the obvious and completely irrelevant fact: "We already have a dog."

I knew this. After three years of work and training, we had only recently settled into a place of relative peace and routine with Jack, but none of that mattered when I thought about Tonka! I talked about him incessantly, but only to Paul. I knew it wouldn't be right to get the kids excited if he wasn't. I don't know what I actually could have talked about, since my knowledge of Tonka was limited to the fact that he was (1) fat, (2) friendly, (3) good with other dogs and children, and (4) housebroken. What more was there to know or to recommend? I was in love.

And yet, I had been a responsible dog owner for three years, and I knew I needed to do some more reading. My newfound passion for the breed was quickly confirmed: "sweet, comical, and charming: the life of the party"; "pugs don't suffer the 'Napoleon complex' common in other small breeds"; "clownlike." I read about their curly little tails that wag in a circular motion and about their snorting and sneezing and funny little barks. I liked everything I read, and then I came across an article titled "Don't Get a Pug."*

It was on a pug rescue site, so I assumed it was written tongue in cheek, one of those "if you can't stand constant love and devotion, don't get a pug." But no, it had some actual warnings, quite a few actually, beginning with *Health Issues*. Apparently pugs are "prone to a myriad of genetic health issues. Be prepared to make a lot of trips to the vet." Well, we had certainly done that with Jack.

There was more.

---

*Pug Village, "Don't Get a Pug," www.pugvillage.com/general/dont-get-pug (accessed January 6, 2016).

Shedding. Pugs shed a lot. "Tons. If you get a pug, you'll have fur all over the place—on every piece of furniture, on all your clothes, and in your car. You don't even have to put your pug in the car; the fur will just be there." Again, I was experienced. I knew *all* about shedding with a big black Lab. How much fur could a dog a quarter of his size really produce?

Housetraining. The article said pugs aren't easy to train, and the process often takes more than a year. "If the idea of a year's worth of poop and pee on the carpet isn't tolerable to you, don't get a pug." That was absolutely *not* tolerable to me—it was a good thing Tonka was already housebroken!

At this point, I may have skimmed the rest.

A Pug Is Your Shadow. "A pug will follow you everywhere. Some people find this endearing . . ." I sure would!

Pugs Don't Catch Frisbees. "Pugs are low-activity dogs . . ." I am a low-activity human!

Pugs Are Indoor Dogs. "Stated quite simply, pugs cannot tolerate high temperatures and humidity." Neither could I!

Pug Maintenance. Pugs need to be brushed frequently. Their facial folds need cleaning. Something about anal sacs, blah, blah, blah . . .

I had given the breed a hard look, and all the "cons" seemed minimal to the numerous "pros." There was no comparison.

I asked Paul whether he minded if I checked in with the rescue—you know, just inquiring about adoption—and by some miracle, he agreed. When I contacted them, the rescue said the first step was to fill out their application. Again I checked with Paul, and again he agreed. This made me feel free to show Tonka's picture to Christopher and Lydia, but I warned them not to say anything to Eden until we were sure everything was a go. She was so young and such a passionate animal lover that I knew it would be too disappointing if we didn't get him. Christopher and Lydia were immediately all in.

I emailed the director of the rescue to express interest, and that's when things started to go sideways.

As I filled out the paperwork, with Lydia perched beside me at the kitchen table, it was impossible to tell who was more thrilled. Then Paul walked in.

"Daddy, aren't you excited about Tonka?" Lydia said.

"Not really."

"Daddy! Why not? Don't you love him?"

"It's not about whether or not I love him. Getting a dog is a big responsibility."

Lydia shrugged.

"Just think about Jack. It's not just the money to acquire the dog; it's also how much we'll spend over his lifetime, and if Tonka is anything like Jack, we'll probably want to set some money aside to be prepared for any unanticipated expenses. I've been thinking about it, and if we decide to get Tonka, we should probably hold off on the new floors in the living room."

My head jerked up involuntarily.

When we bought our house, every floor was covered with off-white carpet, and I do mean *every floor*, including the kitchen and the bathrooms. My agreement to buy the house was contingent on our commitment to replace the floors in all of it. We began with fresh carpet in our bedroom and tile in the bathrooms, and we budgeted for hardwood in the kitchen, dining room, and living room, which all flowed into each other. But then a small kitchen renovation turned into tearing everything down to the studs, and our budget for hardwood floors went to a brand-new kitchen. Several years later, a pipe burst under our sink, and when we replaced the kitchen floor, we paid extra and tore out the carpet and extended the hardwood into the dining room and entry, right up to the front door. Now, two years after that and five years after we had made plans in the first place, we had the money set aside to replace the living room's ancient Berber carpet—a project that would finish the main floor.

"Are you saying if we get Tonka, you don't want to go ahead with the work in the living room?"

"I don't think it would be prudent." Paul was matter-of-fact.

My heart sunk. I had been waiting for five years to get rid of that carpet. Add to that the fact that our first home had an aged Berber in the living room. I had waited for almost ten years to replace it—but we sold the house before we had gotten around to it. All told, I had fifteen years in with tired living room carpet, and now that I thought about it, if we hadn't gotten Jack, I could have had new floors within a year or so of moving into the new house. Of course, I didn't regret that great lug, but what had I been thinking when it came to getting a second dog?

Just like that, I was over Tonka. Lydia and Christopher were sad and disappointed, but we still had Jack. Since we had never met Tonka, he had remained somewhat abstract, and—thank God—we never showed him to Eden.

That fall, we tore out the carpet and installed hardwood. While we were at it, we knocked down some decorative beams I had never liked. Unfortunately, the ceiling couldn't be patched, and we had to tear the whole thing out. While we were at that, we decided to replace the inset ceiling lights. We always hired electricians for any electrical work, even the simplest of jobs, because our homes were older and I was the tiniest bit paranoid about fire. This time, it was a necessary precaution, since some faulty wiring needed replacement. Before we knew it, a project that should have been wrapped up before Thanksgiving was pushing up on Christmas.

After the holidays, I began the house-wide purge, going room by room, decluttering and reorganizing everything. It was a busy time, but even so, I kept thinking about Tonka. I had put the application aside, but I couldn't get him out of my mind.

Every week or so, I would check Petfinder as if I was Facebook stalking a crush: tongue lolling, eyes crinkling, fat gut splaying—a wondrous sight. My love was just as strong, but this time I didn't bother Paul.

One day, Eden and I were out driving, and the van was silent. We were stopped at a red light, and I was looking up at the sky, daydreaming about Tonka as usual, when Eden said, "Mama, you know how I like Chihuahuas?"

"Yes, I do, Eden."

"You know, I've been thinking about it, and I think they're sort of a girly breed, and I'm not a girly girl. Do you know any kinds of dogs that are small enough to dress up that aren't so girly?"

It was as if the heavens opened. For a second, I was frozen in wonder, and then I swallowed and said as casually as I could manage, "Well, there are pugs, you know . . . like Beijing."

"Oh yeah!" When we got home, she looked up "pugs" in one of our many dog books, and just like that, another love affair began. I told Paul about our conversation and asked if he minded if Eden and I went on Petfinder and looked at pugs. We now knew what a dangerous move that could be, but he agreed.

Eden was in the pioneer class of our school district's Mandarin Immersion program. It had gotten off to a rocky start, and Eden, a reluctant Chinese scholar, had been trying to drop out since kindergarten. She had taken to abhorring anything Chinese on principle, and so anything Chinese she expressed an interest in—even pugs—was to be encouraged. That night, Eden and I browsed the pugs in our local rescue. Tonka was still there, large and in charge. I didn't say anything—I wouldn't do that to Paul—but Eden is a smart cookie and knew right away this was not a dog to be missed.

I had explained how a rescue worked, and her heart went out to the dogs that were looking for a forever home.

"Maybe someday we could rescue a pug," she said. "I could help earn the money." Without another thought, she began to save her money. After observing a couple of months of unabated love, admiration, and frequent visits to Petfinder.com, Paul gave his blessing to apply to the local pug rescue. Not wanting to get their hopes up quite yet, I waited to tell the kids.

Ecstatic, I searched for Tonka's listing, as I had done on many other occasions. But Tonka was nowhere to be found. Feeling sick, I checked the adopted page, but he wasn't there either. That's when I really began to worry. Losing Tonka to another loving home was much preferable to losing him period. I emailed the director of the rescue to find out for sure whether or not he was adopted and was thankful to learn he had found a home. I was happy for Tonka but heartbroken for us.

"I know pugs are a wonderful breed in general, but there was just something about Tonka," I said to the director.

Gwynne, the director, wrote back, "No, you're right; there was something special about Tonka."

Paul admitted to being relieved.

"I guess it wasn't meant to be," I said.

One week later, when our house went up in flames, there wasn't any doubt.

For me, this changed everything. Insurance battles, PTSD, and rebuilding plans ensured in my mind that we wouldn't be getting a second dog anytime soon, if ever. What I didn't know is that nothing had changed for Eden.

"I'm so glad I opened my bank account," she had said the morning of the fire, and at the time, I simply assumed it was only about the money. She was thinking about it in a very specific way. That money was her Pug Fund. As she watched our house burn, she was thinking of her pug.

eight

For the Children's Sake

A house fire is the pinup girl of personal tragedy. It gets a lot of attention. People come out of the woodwork to help because a fire taps a literally elemental fear. It's horrible and shocking, but (for those on the outside, at least) the victims' needs seem obvious and manageable—it's a disaster that appears to have an end date.

People were extraordinarily generous and kind. Our house was still smoking when donations began to pour in. Within hours, friends and acquaintances began to rally, and a local business was established as a drop-off point. "What do you need?" we were asked again and again.

You would think it would have been a dream come true to have people lining up to give us stuff. We were incredibly gratified by the extraordinary kindness and generosity of our community—many who were complete strangers—but it was also overwhelming and surprisingly uncomfortable. I thought everything should go to people who were truly in need.

We're fine, I thought. "Do people know we were insured?" I asked Paul more than once.

I was reflexively deflecting help until I remembered a long-ago conversation I had with my next-door neighbor Becky when she was undergoing chemotherapy. I was trying to think of something I could do to help her. "Anything anyone does for my kids helps *me*," she said.

We had lost thousands of books, and my kids were already asking about getting to the library. "Gift cards to bookstores for the children," I said the next time someone asked what they could give.

I asked the kids to make a list of other places we could suggest for people who wanted to buy gift certificates. Christopher and Lydia felt equally excited and awkward. On the one hand, it was fun to be given things, but on the other, it was uncomfortable to be the recipient of charity. Both wrote the names of a few stores without giving it a lot of thought, but Eden made a list that got right to the heart of her loss:

25¢ [Most of her money was in the savings account she had just opened at the credit union, but she had kept back a quarter.]

TIGER BOOK [The night before the fire, we began reading *The Tiger Rising* by Kate DiCamillo, a book about grief and loss.]

SHTRS

PANS

CLTHING [Eden had run out of her burning home in only an oversized T-shirt and a pair of flip-flops, so a new wardrobe was a given.]

LIFE [This one pressed the air out of my chest. I wished you could replace that with a gift card.]

STUFF [She didn't have the strength to list her art supplies and stuffed animals and jewelry and lip gloss, the rest of her books, her toys—but I knew what she meant.]

She circled her top three on the list: the 25¢, the book, and her life.

At first, I tried to pin her down to specific stores. Target? Old Navy? She didn't really care. And then I got it. The child had said what she needed, so I gave her a quarter and called my friend, Jane, who ran out and bought *The Tiger Rising* that day. Clothes came flooding in, along with toys and art supplies and a fat stack of gift cards. But what about her life?

You can't say, "This is it, baby." You can't tell a child there's no going home again, that she's never going back into the safe cocoon that was her life before someone set it, and her house, on fire.

Paul and I knew we needed to tell the children it had been arson. It's bad enough to have something terrible happen to your family, and even worse when other people know more about it than you do. Things have a way of coming out, and then there's a sense of betrayal on top of the wound.

How do you tell children someone *set* their home on fire? They don't cover that in the parenting books. With the loss of the house, we knew our children lost their perception of invulnerability, but I was afraid after we told them it was arson, they would also lose their home in what they believed was a good and safe world.

We decided to tell the big kids first. They would be more prone to hear about it from others, and we wanted to protect Eden as long as possible.

Paul and I sat the older two down and explained about the open car door and the raised door on the corresponding side of the garage. We didn't mention the missing gas can; we just said it looked like it *may* not have been an accident, but we didn't know for sure. We purposely didn't use the term *arson*. We tried to give them just enough information so they wouldn't be sideswiped if they heard the speculation elsewhere, but we tried to keep it to mere possibility.

"Maybe someone was drinking and he wandered into our driveway and opened Daddy's car looking for change and happened to open the garage door and maybe then he stumbled into the garage while smoking a cigarette and accidentally started the fire."

I knew this sounded ludicrous, but a stupid drunk, while implausible, was more palatable than someone who chose our house and purposely set it on fire. And who could believe either scenario? I still couldn't comprehend that my house had burned down, let alone that someone did it.

Christopher shut his eyes. His chin dropped to his chest.

"What are you thinking, buddy?"

He looked up. Tears were already in the corners of his eyes. "I guess I'm shocked," he whispered, and his voice broke.

"How could someone do that?" Lydia, our rule abider, was livid.

"People are careless," I said. "But listen, we don't know what happened, and I would hate for you to get yourself all worked up when we don't know the whole story." Anger had so often ruled my life. I didn't want that for her.

Lydia narrowed her eyes but didn't say anything else.

"We haven't told Eden," Paul said. "We would rather keep this from her until we know more."

Both children nodded. They understood the need to protect their little sister. Eventually, when it came time to tell Eden, she was surprisingly nonchalant. "I thought so! Lydia and Hope thought it started from things rubbing together, but *I* thought someone had to have lit a match." I knew this was just the beginning, that we would need to address this further, but for the time being, I was relieved she took it in stride.

Parenting traumatized kids, as far as I could tell, was just like everyday parenthood in that each child had his or her unique and diverse needs and responses. This was exhausting for Paul and me to keep tabs on, and even more so because we knew how important it was.

Starting out as parents with a child with special needs meant that things had always been complicated. Christopher was a darling baby and an adorable little boy, and yet his many developmental delays and years of diagnoses and therapies, not to mention the surgery for the cochlear implant with complications following it, had required so much from us, sometimes more than we thought we had.

Lydia was bright and precocious and always did well at home and in school. When she became an adolescent with some of the typical behavioral challenges, it was so much harder than I could have imagined. I became terribly aware of how much I had been relying on her near perfection.

Almost every day, we were in a fight, and it was so exhausting and discouraging, because as her character flaws began to emerge, I recognized that she had learned almost every single one from me.

"How *dare* you speak to me like that?" I would shout in the same unloving tone she had used.

When I was a girl, I knew my parents loved me deeply, but I also got the impression they thought there was something inherently wrong that I needed to fix if I expected to be completely accepted. I just didn't know how. I was ashamed of my failings but felt powerless to correct them. Once, in a tearful and angry exchange with Lydia, this memory of hopelessness and shame returned to me. I apologized for shouting at her, and she apologized for being disrespectful. We hugged, as we always do when we reconcile, but she continued to sob. I felt her despair and remembered my own, and something occurred to me.

"Have you ever been a tween before?" I asked.

Lydia stopped mid-sob and looked at me. "No, how could I? That's impossible."

"Well, I've never been the mother of a tween girl before, and I don't know what I'm doing. Do you know what you're doing?"

She shook her head.

"Well, I'm going to learn, and in the meantime, I'm not giving up on you. Are you going to give up on me?"

Lydia was breathing now in shuddery breaths. "No."

I pulled her to me, and she began to cry again. I hugged her and kissed her and told her how glad I was that she's my girl, how thankful I was to be her mom.

It was a turning point for us. We still struggled. We still fought, but something fundamental had shifted into place and solidified beneath our feet. We were committed to each other. We would figure this out together.

There is no good time to have an arsonist set your house on fire, but when you are a twelve-year-old girl, it has got to be one of the worst things to go through. Lydia coped by directing her rage and sorrow into anger and frustration with Paul and me.

The fire was on a Sunday morning, and I called one of our pastors right away. She was able to share the news with the congregation, and they all prayed for us. When we attended church the following Sunday, Pastor Joy asked if we would be willing to come up front during the service to give an update and so they could pray for us in person. Paul and I said, "Yes, of course."

We told the children we were going to go forward. "You can come up with us or stay right here. It's only going to be a couple minutes. Whatever you feel comfortable doing is just fine." Lydia rolled her eyes. She was staying put, and her siblings decided to follow her lead.

But when Pastor Joy invited us up, the children—Lydia included—followed. We lined up on stage, all of them sandwiched between Paul and me. Joy offered the mike, and Paul and I looked at each other. Neither of us has any qualms about public speaking, and I am always happy to talk, but I heard this internal and inexplicable, "Hush."

It was only a week after the fire, and already I had been told over and over what our story was. "You are living a nightmare." That's what people said again and again. "A house fire is my nightmare." I knew they meant losing all their possessions, but that had never been my personal dread, and now that it had happened, it still didn't feel like the worst thing that had happened to us.

I felt this reluctance to speak about it, but not for the reason you may think. When something bad happens to a person of faith, many people wonder, *Do you still believe?* Most don't say it out loud—the question is usually unspoken—but it's palpably present. I did believe. My faith was strong, and God was still good. The burden still felt light, and I didn't know how to talk about it in a way that didn't make me appear to be more than I was. I thought it would be like asking a naturally thin person who never exercised and could eat whatever she wanted to speak at a Weight Watcher's meeting.

Paul said a few words about how we were amazed by and so thankful for the outpouring of support, keeping it short and sincere, before reaching across the children to hand the mike to me.

When it passed in front of Lydia, she grabbed it and clutched it to her chest.

She paused and swallowed hard. I stared, my eyes never wider. I had no idea what she was going to say.

"The day of the fire, my dad said, 'Lydia, God takes ashes and gives beauty'"—a sharp sob stopped her.

"All right!" someone in the congregation shouted in encouragement.

Lydia breathed in. The church was quiet, and I could feel the congregation hanging on, completely with and for my girl. " . . . and I'm going to try to trust him." Lydia exhaled.

It was clear she couldn't say anything else. She handed me the mike, which I passed right back to Pastor Joy. Tears were streaming down my face. Even if I had wanted to say something, I knew that moment had passed. I couldn't speak, and besides, nothing else needed to be said.

The church erupted in cheers and clapping. I heard our senior pastor, Pastor Dave, shout from the front row, "Yay, Lydia!"

In the car after church, I turned around to face her. "Do you know you had a powerful opportunity today?"

"What do you mean?"

"Did you notice how quiet it got when you were talking?"

She nodded.

"After a tragedy, when a child talks, everyone listens intently. For one, their hearts are with you because they are being kind and caring, but in another way, they are listening on behalf of the children they once were. They are listening with their own sorrows and heartaches, and today you had the chance to speak for them. That's why I didn't say anything afterward. You said everything that needed to be said."

"Thank you, Mama," she said, crying again.

I looked at her and could only nod. I was crying too.

Later at Dawn and Thom's, Lydia found me in my room alone.

"I'm sorry I've been such a brat," she said.

"Honey, we're all under a lot of stress."

"I know. But that's not an excuse."

I wasn't making an excuse for her, merely acknowledging the truth.

"It's like everything, honey. We don't know what we're doing; you're a tween who's never had your house burn down, and I've never mothered a tween whose house just burned down, but we're learning." This was so absurd, and we both laughed through our tears.

We were taking this crash course together. And together, we'd find our way.

In parenthood there is always an invitation to exercise surrender and faith and, at the same time, a call to hold on tenaciously. Holding on and letting go is the continual and impossible assignment. Navigating which situation calls for which is where things get tricky. Of course, trust is *always* needed; even before the fire, it was clear I did not have life under control. It is painful to see your children hurt and to know that all you can do is listen and pray and offer your faith on their behalf, which *is* so very much but—in the short term anyway—doesn't feel like enough.

And there was this other tricky thing: Whether or not we recognized it, Paul and I were traumatized too.

nine

A Tiny Case of Post-Traumatic Stress

After Paul and I met with the adjuster, Torey picked me up to take me to get a few things. We first stopped at our local health food store. I was on a mission to find something—anything—to help me sleep.

I felt a sudden euphoria as I pushed my cart around Harvest Health, merely by virtue of the fact that I was no longer at my burned-out house. I felt free and easy—away from the smoke stains, Stan's suspicions, and Bob's terrible jokes. If the packaging read "sleep aid" or "stress relief," I grabbed the biggest bottle. I even found some expensive drops that promised to alleviate stress eating. *For such a time as this*, I thought, and tossed them in the cart.

The cashier rang up bottle after bottle, totaling more than $100. Since I no longer owned a wallet, I pulled the Red Cross credit card straight out of my FedEx tote bag. These subtleties were lost on the cashier.

"Wow," she said, "you're going to be feeling good!"

She was young, but it seems to me that someone purchasing $100 worth of stress and sleep aids is obviously a person under extreme duress.

"Oh yeah!" I said with enthusiasm and hoped she was right.

Getting my computer checked out was next on the list. At the Apple store, a young man with an iPad immediately approached. "Terrence," his name tag read.

"How can I help you today?" he asked.

"I need to buy a cord for my laptop," I said. My mind flashed to those last moments in the house—fire alarms blaring, jamming my computer in its bag, running barefoot out of the house. I saw my study as it now was—ceiling and roof burned away, the walls charred, the cord probably buried under the ruins of the sofa or ceiling—a scene that couldn't be further away from the white and bright atmosphere of an Apple store.

82

"Great!" Terrence was clearly committed to getting me the help I needed. "Let me get your name to have you meet with a Genius. There are quite a few people with appointments, so it's going to be a little while."

That wasn't going to work for me. I had a long list of things to buy, and I was beginning to realize that being out and about in a world where people had intact houses filled with actual purses and wallets, not to mention bras that fit, felt like a parallel universe and was more than a little disconcerting—no, it was untenable.

I suddenly realized I was holding a fast pass—and it was the fast pass to trump all fast passes. We certainly can't control the cards we are dealt—goodness knows—and although my brain hadn't yet formulated the idea of there being a "fire card," I was about to play it for the very first time.

I just couldn't do it in front of Torey.

Feeling the situation required a certain delicacy, I turned slightly to the side so it was just Terrence and me, huddled tête-à-tête next to a wall display of iPhones.

Despite my distinct weirdness, Terrence was indefatigably polite, and I could tell he was committed to administering excellent Apple care to even the strangest customer. He bent his head toward mine.

"My house burned down," I said gently, not wanting to frighten him.

Terrence blanched.

I nodded. It was shocking, but we needed to soldier on.

"My laptop is the only thing I was able to save. I lost the cord, and even before the fire, I needed to bring it in to be looked at. The casing has pulled away, and I want to make sure everything is working properly."

Terrence swallowed hard.

"I'm going to talk to a Genius," he said, then whisked away. Torey and I watched him pull one of the guys aside. They looked over, and I smiled reassuringly. *Yes, it's me; I'm the Fire Lady.*

Torey decided to divide and conquer. "You take care of things here, and I'll head over to J.Crew to see what they have and maybe pick out some things for you to try on."

Playing the fire card was a success; within minutes, James was taking a look at my laptop.

"This casing was a manufacturing flaw. We can replace that for you free of charge."

"How long will it take?"

"Oh," he said as he looked at the repair schedule, "probably a day or two at the most."

The thought of leaving my computer was worrisome. I leaned close and spoke in an undertone.

"I lost everything, including all my pictures and videos, except this laptop and what's on it. I really need everything to be safe. What do I need to do?"

"It's quite safe—" He stopped. "I usually say, 'Unless the mall burned down.'" He looked me in the eye, and I smiled.

"Do you have an external hard drive?" he asked.

I shook my head. "Not anymore."

His face flashed with the embarrassment. That pesky fire!

"OK. Let's get you a new one, and I'll back everything up onto it right now so you can have that before you leave." I exhaled. That worked.

We stood together quietly while everything loaded.

"You know fires are incredibly common. One in ten homes is affected by a fire," I said. It had come to this. Fire statistics were my new small talk.

The Genius standing next to James overheard.

"Whoa! Kinda depressing! What's up with this talk about fires?"

In my experience, Apple Geniuses tend to fall into two categories. First, there's the competent and matter-of-fact dude who takes care of your needs quickly and efficiently without any fanfare. Then there's the younger, cockier type, for whom the title Genius isn't worn tongue in cheek but heavily, with deep self-regard. James, being a member of the former category, shut his eyes for a second and winced. I knew he felt terrible for me, but I was fine. I did appreciate his compassion and wanted to pat him on the back to let him know I had this under control. Because just then I realized the fire card wasn't just a card; at times it was a hammer, and I was about to lower it. Hard.

I smiled at the Genius next over, clearly one who occupied the latter category. "Well, my house burned down two days ago, and it *is* 'kinda depressing.'"

Next Over Genius's mouth dropped open. "I'm so sorry . . . I had no idea—"

I waved away his apologies. Of course he didn't know. I may have been wearing a borrowed and ill-fitting bra. My feet might have been slightly smudged with ash, but I hitched my FedEx tote bag high on my shoulder and stood up straight. All these things were true. And yes, I had lost everything, but I still had my pride.

With external hard drive in hand, I met Torey outside Macy's, wherein I surrendered to the tape measure and tender ministrations of one of the older ladies who has fitted me with bras over the years since my first pregnancy. Soon the too small T-shirt was stretched over my perky and properly supported chest. Blessed progress.

Next stop was J.Crew, where Torey had set aside a nice pair of jeans and a few shirts. By some miracle, everything fit, and I paid for it all with my Red Cross Visa card. Torey wanted to head to Banana Republic too, but a great weariness suddenly descended, and I just wanted to get back home—as I had already begun to think of Dawn and Thom's. I was so exhausted I could barely make it out to her car.

As we headed north, a car full of young men buzzed past us, and I thought I saw the driver texting.

Just like that, I was wide-awake.

I whacked Torey on the arm and yelled. "I think that guy was texting," I said. "That's against the law now. Speed up! Let's get his license plate."

Torey's sister-in-law, who was getting her master's in counseling, had already warned her that our family might experience PTSD, but this was the first time Torey really saw it in action.

"Give me your phone," I demanded. Mine had burned in the fire, and the replacement from Verizon hadn't yet arrived.

"It's in my purse," she said, glancing at me with wide and nervous eyes.

"This is 911. What's your emergency?"

"Yes. Hello. A car just raced past us, and the driver was driving erratically. I believe he was texting. We're headed north on the Beltline, just south of Lake. We're coming up on Lake. It's a white Accord, probably mid-90s. I wasn't able to get the license plate—oh, we're north of Lake now. I can just see them ahead of us."

The 911 dispatcher thanked me for the information, but I got the sense that she wasn't rushing to send out an all points bulletin. After I hung up, Torey was quiet for a moment.

"I think maybe you need to talk to somebody?" It was a statement, but her voice lifted up like it was a question. I knew she was treating me gently, as if I was acting unbalanced. But I knew I was being perfectly balanced. Those boys were a threat. They needed to be stopped. I was helping keep things safe.

I didn't try to explain, and Torey didn't challenge me. Her silence should have told me how worried she was, but I didn't notice. I was fine. My laptop was getting fixed. I had new jeans, a couple of cute shirts, and bras that actually fit. I had a whole bag full of herbal solutions for all my sleeping, de-stressing, happy-making needs. I was making my comeback quite nicely. Or so I thought.

"Two to three weeks." That's what the insurance adjuster had said it would take before the shock would wear off.

"Are you even angry?" Dawn asked me, a week or so later.

I thought for a moment. "I don't think so," I said. "Not yet."

She shook her head, with tears in her eyes. "I can't believe how well you're doing."

I knew everyone thought I was being a brave little soldier, but I didn't feel like one. I felt like myself—just an extremely tired and slightly shattered version of me. But I wasn't angry, and losing everything still didn't feel as painful as other people assumed it was.

Two weeks and six days after the fire—that was how we were all keeping time now—I was scheduled to meet with a landscaper hired by the public adjuster to appraise our landscaping claim. I arrived at the house first.

Nothing can really accustom you to the sight of your half-burned house. It's not something you can get used to. It's a shock every time.

I pulled into the driveway behind our burned-out van. I got out and walked around while I waited. It was quiet and peaceful. I had begun to garden soon after I became a homeowner. I knew nothing. I couldn't even remember the difference between annuals and perennials. Plants that came back every year should be annuals, right?

I became a true gardener during a time of great duress. It became important that next summer as Christopher was being diagnosed and misdiagnosed. I was pregnant with Lydia, who was a bit of a surprise, and it was a hard pregnancy. I couldn't control my little boy's health and my own fertility, but darn it, I could control a bed of irises and a planting of hostas. I was an unstoppable force. As soon as Christopher went down for a nap or when Paul was home to be with him, I was working in my yard, digging new beds and planting nonstop. There is something deeply elemental to digging in the dirt and feeling its cool richness between your fingers—although I religiously wore gloves because I was pregnant and knew that birth defects were for real.

Years later, in our second home, I ripped out shrubs and perennials I didn't like and enlarged existing beds. I created an entirely new one that extended from the gazebo in a large pie shape down to the driveway. In front of the gazebo, I built a large teepee from branches and wove twine in and over and then planted green beans and morning glories to grow up it. I lined the whole bed with small boulders and made several paths across the bed so the kids could run through it. It became, unofficially, the children's garden, and Eden, a gardener in her own right, its little queen.

It had somewhat survived the fire. The teepee was still standing, but the fire's heat had killed all the vines. A little cardboard star Eden had painted and tied from a string to the top of the teepee slowly twisted back and forth in the soft breeze.

After a bit, the landscaper arrived.

"I've never really done this before," he said. This was a red flag, but I missed it. This was my first fire too.

"I think we should start with the trees," he suggested.

Our house was set in a valley. To the west and the south were steep, wooded hills. Several tall and beautiful maples grew throughout the front and side yards. All of them sheltered the house and turned brilliant colors in the fall. The largest was just outside our bedroom window, and most heavily hit. I knew that one wasn't going to make it. Another was in the middle of the front yard—the one that Paul and I had tried to cut down the first year we lived in the house, until we casually mentioned it to Lydia.

"Not the climbing tree!"

We didn't know there *was* a climbing tree. But sure enough, it was the one in the center of the yard that turned colors late in the season, so we were raking almost into winter. It had divided into three trunks, making it ideal for getting a foothold. Who could cut down a child's climbing tree? Not us. It was only half burned, but the landscaper didn't think it could be saved.

The maple closest to the house was also gone. Anyone could see that, as was the maple just to the west of the driveway. The Japanese maple near the front door—a sad little stalk.

The landscaper carefully marked them in his notebook.

"I think this one will be able to recover," he said, indicating yet another maple that grew about halfway down the hill—the one that had always sheltered our gazebo and that I especially loved. Once the trees were all noted, we moved on to the garden beds. The worst hit were the large foundational plantings in front and along the west side, next to the garage. Everything was gone. Since I had planted every single shrub and perennial, I had a fairly strong grasp on what was missing. We walked slowly around, and I named what had been lost and estimated how many of each, since many were multiple plantings.

I noted the ferns I had been trying to naturalize. The morning before the fire, I had counted them, as was my daily practice. All now lost.

I named the many hostas, noting the specimens. The landscaper made a quick sketch and wrote down everything I said.

"OK," he said, looking at his sheet, "I'm pricing the hostas at five dollars apiece."

I was stunned.

"They were huge," I said. "Most of them were at least five years old. They *dappled*." I leaned forward, boring this hard fact into him.

He was clearly unmoved. But he looked up from his paper and squinted at me.

"You know you're going to have to start over, right?"

We were standing in my ravaged yard, in front of my burned-out house. Of all people, I knew I was going to have to start over. Yes, as a matter of fact, I did.

We were finished in more ways than one. I was enraged. I immediately called the public adjuster to let him know we were going to have to hire someone else. I remembered the landscapers we had used when we planted some white spruce when we first bought the house. I couldn't remember the name offhand, but they had designed a couple of the public gardens in our little town and engraved their name on a decorative stone. I could just drive by and read it. I'd do it right away.

The next morning was a Sunday, three weeks to the day of the fire. I woke up around four thirty and couldn't get back to sleep. Paul got up a little before seven to go early to church to lead singing with a group. This annoyed me.

"I guess I thought you would have canceled going, at least for this month," I said.

"Well, I didn't, so they're planning on me, and I'd like to go."

I would have thought he would have taken time off since we were living on the edge. It didn't occur to me that this was a haven for him, a release of stress. Or if it did, it was secondary to the fact that it increased my own. I just didn't want to face anything without Paul. And I felt overwhelmed by church. People were concerned and wanted to touch base—even people we barely knew. This was loving and caring, yet draining. Everyone asked how we were doing, which was so kind, but there were always questions about the fire, which was upsetting for the children and exhausting for me. Being an introvert, if there was a way to be airlifted into church and then out again immediately after, that would be my preference many a Sunday, but especially three weeks after an arsonist set my house on fire.

Paul left, and a half hour later, the rest of us piled—grumbling—into the car.

There were several ways to get to church, but I chose the quickest and most familiar route, which brought us past the house. About a mile away, I began to feel my exhaustion. I was so tired.

We crested the hill. I reached our intersection and stopped at the sign. We all looked, but no one said anything. The sight of our ruined home was like a body blow. I should have gone a different way. I should have spared my children this. *Why didn't I take a different route?* I was so tired that I could barely keep my head up. The thought of driving all the way to church, answering the questions of all the caring and concerned people, and then sitting through the service felt impossible.

"Kids," I announced, "we're not going to church!"

No one cheered, but there was a collective and relieved exhalation.

I thought of the landscaper. This would be the perfect time to stop by the public garden and get the name of the nursery.

I turned into town and slowly drove by the garden. The engraving on the rock had softened over the years, and I couldn't read it at first glance. It was early Sunday morning in the summer, and the roads were deserted, so I stopped the van and squinted. It was on the right side, so I leaned across Lydia in the passenger seat.

"Can you read that?" All three children peered with me, and we read it out loud.

"Roods?"

"Rooks?"

Something clicked. *That's it. Rooks.* It felt like a small victory.

"Well done!" I shouted to the back and began taking my foot off the brake.

I heard a shout and turned to see several cyclists passing me on the left, and one was right beside my door. I slammed on the brakes and rolled down my window.

Later I will figure out what must have happened. They came up behind me and paused. When I didn't move, they started to pass me just as I began to pull forward. I should have looked around before I accelerated.

"Hey!" one of them yelled, much too close to the van. His face was red and angry.

Horrified at my mistake, I rolled down my window to apologize.

"I'm so—" I began to say, but he waved me away, as if to shut me up and rode off.

I will be honest. I always like to be heard. Anyone who has argued with me knows I can be . . . tenacious. So there's that. I really didn't like being cut off when I knew I was wrong and was trying to do the right thing.

Also, I was what the professionals call "raw."

I stepped on the gas.

"Mama!" Lydia shouted, and I could feel the general anxiety of all the children. But justice was calling.

Tires squealed as I pulled up next to the cyclist. I rolled down Lydia's window. He looked up, surprised.

"Mama—," Eden said.

"I was trying to say I'm sorry," I began.

He shrugged me off and kept riding. This did not work for me.

"I'm sorry I was stopped in the middle of the road. I'm SORRY I didn't see you because I was trying to read a landscaper's sign because an ARSONIST BURNED MY HOUSE DOWN!"

The cyclist's face changed. I can only imagine what mine looked like, but right then, I was past caring.

"Lady," he said, "we're OK." He held out the arm nearest me in a gesture of pacification, but this—or simply the fact that he was completely wrong—set me off.

"WE ARE NOT OK!" I shrieked and stomped on the gas pedal, speeding past him. The children were screaming now. I turned into the nearest parking lot and slammed to a stop. For a moment it was mostly quiet, except for my sobbing and the kids catching their breath.

I felt so ashamed. I was a terrible mother.

"I'm so sorry." I turned to them. "I'm sorry I lost it."

"That guy was a jerk," Christopher said.

"Yeah, he was. But I shouldn't have freaked out and driven so recklessly."

"No, you shouldn't have," Eden said primly.

"You sure freaked out all right," Lydia said. I turned to look at her. Her eyes were wide, and then she smiled. It was a nervous smile, but it was a smile, and I smiled back. We both began to laugh.

"We are not OK!" Eden imitated my screech, and soon we were all laughing.

I still felt terrible. "I'm so, so sorry, guys. Will you please forgive me?"

There was a murmur of "I forgive you" from all three. I looked at them. Tears welled up in my eyes. My throat was sore from screaming, a shameful reminder.

There was plenty to rationalize if I wanted. I *was* exhausted and had been startled. That guy *was* a jerk. And maybe there was something to that talk about post-traumatic stress. All that was real and valid, but it didn't change the fact that I had been wrong and had wronged another. I had certainly wronged my children.

There was no way to make amends with the cyclist, which I had genuinely wanted to do at the start until I tilted into a rage at his blow-off of my apology. But now, again, I truly wanted to apologize.

I had made it right with my children, but it didn't feel like it. Not yet.

The funny thing about grace is that even though I know it covers every wrong, it rarely feels like enough. At least in the short term, especially when I've sinned before and against my children. Time and maturity had taught me the only thing I can do is open my arms to lay down my shame and keep them open to receive forgiveness. There is no plan B. All I know is to admit my wrongdoing and then accept grace when it's given, *especially* when it doesn't feel like enough.

I looked at my children, one by one, and they looked back at me.

"Thank you" was all I could say, and then I turned the van around and drove slowly and carefully back to Dawn and Thom's—to home.

ten

A Time to Tear Down

Several months before the fire, Eden and I had read *The Jesus Storybook Bible* together. Every night at bedtime, we snuggled in her bed, and I read aloud one of the stories. Eden, for obvious reasons, had always loved reading about the Garden of Eden in the Bible or hearing it mentioned in church. In *The Jesus Storybook Bible*, it was called Adam and Eve's "perfect home," but she knew what it truly was and listened attentively. I read the stories slowly, enjoying the rich language, and I found myself moved as well. Especially when we got to the part where Adam and Eve have eaten the apple, despite God telling them not to, and he is explaining the consequences.

> "You will have to leave the garden now," God told his children, his eyes filling with tears. "This is no longer your true home, it's not the place for you anymore."
>
> But before they left the garden, God made clothes for his children, to cover them. He gently clothed them and then he sent them away on a long, long journey—out of the garden, out of their home.
>
> Well, in another story, it would all be over and that would have been . . .
>
> The End.
>
> But not in this Story.[*]

I felt a thrill when I read this. I was struck by the beauty of the gospel. Because of it, we get to tell—we get to live—another story.

> God loved his children too much to let the story end there. Even though he knew he would suffer, God had a plan—a magnificent dream. One day, he would get his children back. One day, he would make the world their perfect home again. And one day, he would wipe away every tear from their eyes.

---

[*]Sally Lloyd-Jones, *The Jesus Storybook Bible* (Grand Rapids: Zondervan, 2007), 34–35.

You see, no matter what, in spite of everything, God would love his children—with a Never Stopping, Never Giving Up, Unbreaking, Always and Forever Love.

And though they would forget him, and run from him, deep in their hearts, God's children would miss him always, and long for him—lost children yearning for their home.

Before they left the garden, God whispered a promise to Adam and Eve: "It will not always be so! I will come to rescue you! And when I do, I'm going to do battle against the snake. I'll get rid of the sin and the dark and the sadness you let in here. I'm coming back for you!"

And he would. One day, God himself would come.*

"That's not true," Eden said. I looked at her, surprised. It was literally gospel truth. What was her problem?

"What do you mean?"

"There's still crying and sadness. It's not gone."

I thought for a moment. When talking about spiritual matters with my children, I have always tried to avoid easy, tossed-off answers.

"But the story isn't over," I said. Eden looked at me. "We're in the story," I said and realized, even as I was saying it, that I was explaining this to myself.

I'm rarely aware of it, just like most people. I'm busy living my life, and in trying to be a decent wife, mother, sister, daughter, friend, and neighbor, I sometimes get lost in the day-to-day. I forget I'm a part of something larger, something so big and long it stretches back in time to the ancient of days, but every once in a while, I'm pulled out of the mundane and I remember: We're in the middle of the story.

That was exactly how I felt in the earliest days after the fire. It was like a big book had cracked open, and I was a character right in the middle of the most fascinating—at times, terrifying—story, and I couldn't wait to see what might happen next.

I've always loved that one of the names of Jesus is Immanuel, which in Hebrew means "God with us." The entire Christian faith rests on the idea that he descended from heaven and "made his dwelling among us"

---

*Ibid., 36.

and continues, through the Holy Spirit, to be with us. But what does that mean? For more than a year before the fire I had been thinking about that. Afterward, I had the sense God was going to reveal all my spiritual and emotional detritus, and like the trash pile that began the actual fire, it was all going to burn away. In the early days of shock when I felt strangely free, this wasn't alarming. I guess I thought, just like during the real fire, it wasn't going to hurt, and I wondered if all the other hard times we had been through had prepared us for this. *Maybe, just maybe*, a quiet part of me wondered, *this is what spiritual maturity feels like.*

This was a spiritual odyssey—of that I was certain—and I knew I was going to come out of it with a profound understanding about the presence of God, *and* (this may have been in the back of my mind) a sparkling new house with stone countertops and a walk-in pantry. It was a win-win if I ever heard of one. I forgot this was only the beginning of a journey, and now as I look back, I can see I thought I knew how the story would end.

I had no idea.

Here's the thing about a house fire, or really any loss: Before you can rebuild, you have to tear down the ruins, and you can't tear them down until you make an inventory. You have to record everything you have lost. You're required—spiritually, emotionally, and materially—to give a reckoning.

Have you seen those insurance commercials where a kindly insurance adjuster appears right on the scene of a disaster, immediately cutting a generous check to the devastated homeowner? I'm sorry to tell you it's not quite like that. Well, maybe it is for a small claim. Before our house burned, we had a pipe burst, which flooded our kitchen, damaging that floor and the floor of the bathroom next to it. The insurance adjuster was easy to work with and wrote us a check (minus our deductible) as soon as we had estimates done.

But with a catastrophic claim, there's just so much room for fraud on a homeowner's part, and for negotiating on the side of insurance.

The day after our first meeting with our insurance adjuster, Paul scheduled an appointment with the first public adjuster—a so-called ambulance chaser—who had contacted us. They called the night of the fire. There was definitely something to the accusation of chasing, but Paul had read the book sent to him by Thom's cousin and, after a lengthy talk with him, had decided hiring a public adjuster was the way to go. I wasn't so sure.

I was raised with the mantra, "There's a right way and a wrong way to do everything." This applied to how to cut carrots and how to invest your life savings—and everything in between. There weren't really margins for growth, or for error. This embedded in me a reluctance to making quick decisions, of any kind, certainly not the "you could be making a mistake that will cost you thousands and thousands of dollars" variety. Also, ever since a bookkeeper embezzled her way through our family business, I had been the teensiest bit jumpy about money, which compounded my hesitancy in making any decision out of fear of making a costly and irrevocable misstep.

Paul met with the public adjuster the day after we met with our insurance adjuster, Bob, but I stayed at Dawn and Thom's. I was exhausted from meeting with Bob and then venturing into civilization, and someone needed to sort through the mountains of donations that were pouring in daily.

Paul came back from the meeting gung ho and ready to sign without a doubt. I was full of doubts. This began a tense couple days while "we" decided. I would probably still be huddled in the fetal position except for the fact that Paul said something that scared me into action.

"Ali, I'm concerned if we continue to wait, doors will begin to close. This isn't open-ended. We have to start making decisions." Just taking the time to try to make a good decision could be a bad decision. There is no winning with a house fire! If you want to pinpoint a time when ours went irrevocably bad for me, beyond the obvious moment when the arsonist lit the match, this would be it.

I agreed to meet with public adjusters and afterward decided Paul was right: it was in our best interest to sign with them. This particular company had worked with Bob on many claims and called him on our behalf to get everything going. The first step was to begin assessing the home's value and to secure temporary housing for us. Thom and Dawn graciously welcomed us indefinitely. The first morning after the fire,

Thom told me, "Ali, don't rush into anything. Dawn and I want you to stay here as long as you need to. This is your home now." That meant everything to Paul and me, and yet, school would be starting in just a couple months, and we would need to be close to the kids' schools. The insurance company hired a temporary housing company to help us find a house to rent while we were rebuilding.

The next task was to assess the value of the structure—the house itself. The public adjuster hired a builder to create an estimate. Since some of the house remained standing, this part of the claim moved relatively quickly.

Valuing the contents of the home was much more belabored. Every single item in the house had to be listed in an inventory. The content specialists came and went through the house, room by room, and shoveled though the wreckage to list every single item that hadn't burned or, even if it did, could still be recognized. This took weeks. When the inventory was finally completed, it was so big it had to be shipped to me in a box, and then my work began. My job was to list anything I knew about every item—the age; the make; the model; whether it was bought new or secondhand or was a gift. At first I couldn't even face it.

I had just spent the last six months going room by room, winnowing through all my possessions, trying to get down to what I thought I couldn't live without—and here I was, finding out I was going to have to live without it all.

When I say I had gone through all our possessions, I mean everything. I even sorted out the boxes of my children's art and mementos. I was able to throw away anything where only gluing was involved, but any drawing or writing—especially "I love you, Mom"—I threw in the KEEP box without a second thought.

I lost almost all my possessions and barely shed a tear, but a month or so later, it finally hit me. We were staying at a friend's cottage, and I was snuggled in bed between Lydia and Eden, tucking them in. I suddenly turned wide-eyed at the thought: Not only did I lose everything my kids ever made me, but none of it could ever be replaced.

My children were growing up. Christopher and Lydia didn't draw me pictures anymore and rarely made me cards. Eden was a loose cannon; the youngest grow up so fast. I thought of all the family portraits they had made. I loved seeing each child's vision of who we were. In the portraits, our bodies might only be big circles, or they might be sophisticated enough to have arms and legs with hands and feet. In some, we floated in the air; in others, we were lined up neatly in order: Paul, me, Christopher, and Lydia—and then, when she came, Eden, and eventually Jack. One consistent thing in every single one is that we all had enormous smiles. In those portraits, nothing got us down.

But then, just weeks after the fire, I lay in that big bed hugging both my girls and thought about how quickly they were growing up, and I began to cry. Through tears, I explained to the girls what I was feeling and then sobbed until my head ached. Soon we were all weeping together. I was still happy to be alive. I still knew the pictures were part of the stuff, which didn't matter as much as the people they represented. I was still unutterably grateful that our family was spared. And yet, in light of all that, I still was sad to lose those precious cards and drawings.

Lydia, who was twelve going on thirty at the time, said, "But, Mom, those cards and pictures and letters weren't us; it's like they were a shadow of us, like an imprint we left behind, but they weren't us. We're still here, and we're going to be telling you we love you for the rest of our lives."

I had read the Bible verses in the book of Ecclesiastes hundreds of times: "There is a time for everything, and a season for every activity under the heavens: a time to be born and a time to die, a time to plant and a time to uproot . . ."* I knew there was a time for weeping and laughing, for mourning and dancing, but it was only after my house burned that "a time to tear down and a time to build" leapt off the page. I had never noticed tearing down came first until I realized how hard it can be.

We eventually settled into a rental just down the road from the house. Every day, Christopher and Lydia rode by it on their bus, and Paul drove by it on his way to work. It was like a corpse. Seeing it day after day, week after week, only increased our sorrow.

People began to complain to the township. The burned-out house

---

*Ecclesiastes 3:1–3.

was an eyesore. When was it going to be removed? We had to wait for the building estimates to be made, the inventory created, and every requirement from the township met before they would issue a demolition permit. You would think they would have these written down to expedite the process—that's what we thought—but no dice. The township doled out the requirements one by one to the builder, who then passed them on to Paul and me, and we scrambled to meet their demands.

The day after the fire, Paul called all the utility companies to request shutoffs in the interests of safety and expense. Six weeks later, I spent hours on the phone with Comcast trying to move our phone number, which we had kept open, forwarding the calls to Dawn and Thom's, in the hope of keeping one small thing stable for my children, but for unfathomable reasons (we were in the same town and area code), they couldn't or wouldn't fulfill our request.

When our builder informed us we needed shutoff notices from each of the utilities, including cable, for the township to issue a demolition permit, we weren't thrilled, especially since we had just spent three weeks getting the gas company to shut off the gas at the street. But what can you do?

The first call to any utility involves a lengthy tour of call prompts. I try to avoid this by hitting 0 for the operator, but it doesn't always work, since their goal is not to promptly get you to where you need to go but to divert you while you wait. The electric company, for example, required the caller to enter the twenty-digit account number. I muttered as I carefully entered all the numbers, but I was delighted to hear a real-live human greeting me almost immediately. The pleasure was short-lived. As soon as I told her what I needed, she asked for my account number.

"I just entered it! What is the point of having people—" I stopped. What *was* the point? I repeated the number.

"Now what is it you need again?"

"The shutoff notice from Consumers Energy." I knew I needed to use the proper terms, as well as the name of her employer. With customer service agents, there seems to be no middle road. They are either friendly, helpful, and efficient, or none of the above and—I'm sorry to be harsh here—dim-witted to boot.

I had already told her we'd had a house fire, which she misconstrued to mean our power had been shut off and I was trying to get it turned back on. I reiterated that we had had no power for months because we had asked them to turn it off after the house burned and now we needed a copy of the shutoff notice in order to get permission to TEAR DOWN THE BURNED-OUT RUINS.

"Oh, you need to speak to an engineer. They are the ones who handle that." She put in a request for one to call me.

I waited two days before I called back. This customer service rep was more helpful.

"It shows the request was made and an engineer has been assigned. Would you like his direct line?"

I would indeed!

My call promptly went into voice mail. Daryn the Engineer was out of the office celebrating Veterans Day. I left a message. The next day, at the end of the day, when I hadn't heard back, I called again. I called again Monday early afternoon and realized he left his cell number on the message. I dialed that number, and he answered! *Daryn!* How I had longed to hear his voice.

It was a terrible connection. I could hear him, but he couldn't hear me. We said hello back and forth several times. His tone was perplexed. Mine was thrilled and ever so slightly demented. "Can you hear me now?" I shouted.

The call was lost. Before I could despair, my phone rang, and it was Daryn!

"HELLO!" I answered.

"Hi, I just got a call from this number . . ."

I explained who I was and why I was calling.

"Oh, OK—yeah." Daryn was no orator, but I hung on his every word. "Um, I just quit my job last night, so you're going to have to call my boss and find out who was assigned your case."

"You're not going to believe this," I said to Paul after I hung up. "Daryn quit his job last night."

"You have got to be kidding me."

Fortunately Daryn's boss assigned me to another engineer, Leslie, who actually seemed to understand the urgency, on so many levels, of having what was left of our home torn down. That afternoon, she ran over to the house, and by evening, the shutoff notice was in my inbox.

We still had the other utilities to deal with and to hassle with—of all things—draining the septic tank, but eventually, finally, by some miracle, the permit was issued and the demolition was scheduled, with nothing standing in the way.

The day was bitterly cold, and a layer of snow covered everything. I was so eager to have it all gone and yet anxious to see it one last time. It was like a strange breakup that had dragged on far too long. On the one hand, I just wanted it over, and on the other, I was, to the bitter end, looking for some kind of closure. The morning of the demolition, after I got the big kids on the bus and dropped off Paul at work and Eden at school, I went back to the rental and walked down to the house.

The ruins had become a common sight, but I tried to pay special attention. I went to the front door and looked in. I thought of the morning of the fire when the flames burned through it and I knew this was no longer home. Then there was the first time we returned to the house and surveyed the damage. I was struck, even more than by what was gone, by what remained. My front door was destroyed. The knob was twisted and partially melted. Two bookcases flanked the front door. Part of the roof of the entry had burned to nothing, but both bookcases were still standing. One was leaning forward, and I had the strong sense of two soldiers, bloodied but unbowed. The top shelf of the case on the east wall had held my collection of vintage Modern Library. I only had a couple dozen or so, but there were some beauties (*Nine Stories* by J. D. Salinger with the dust jacket!), and I loved them. They must have slipped off when the bookcase pitched forward but were covered by my set of Shakespeare, which had fallen together and formed a sort of stepping-stone.

How did the fire go through and over all those books and yet they didn't burn? Every time I visited the house, I would peek in the front door and look at them—artifacts of a life long gone. As time passed, they weathered and aged, and more fell.

And now it was time to say good-bye altogether.

Waiting for the excavator to arrive, I walked around the house and tried to see everything one last time. I took some pictures, and then I made my way to my perch on the hill, where I sat and watched them tear the house down, as one might sit and watch fireworks.

The demolition began at 10:33 in the morning with a gentle tap to Jack's doghouse, which caused it to crack and then fly apart like a house of cards.

I had never seen a building torn down and had imagined it would be loud and, well, destructive, but it was a surprisingly delicate operation. The scoop of the excavator gently knocked and nibbled its way through the structure. It was like a hand carefully plucking and rearranging, but instead of straightening or fixing, it was tearing apart.

It was strange seeing familiar things fly to the surface and land on the top of the pile: the antique metal box I used for storage on the bathroom counter, a vintage housecoat the girls wore for dress-up, Lydia's lavender parka from a few years ago that I was saving for Eden, the granite on my island, one of my living room chairs, a green cereal bowl.

It was a little like watching a slideshow at a funeral, where, for a moment, you forget the loss and lovingly remember.

It was finished fifty-seven minutes later, after a delicate pull at the southwest corner of the laundry room. The walls came down, and then they were pulled up and added to the top of the pile. The ivy that grew along the foundation was pulled up too and, still attached, trailed along.

When only the laundry room stood—even its roof was gone—I found myself sitting up and leaning forward, like at the end of a movie, but there wasn't any suspense, just the sense of something long awaited finally coming to an end.

The house had stood for more than fifty years, and we had lived in it for six. It took less than an hour to demolish the structure, and two days to haul away the massive pile of rubbish. Isn't that the way of things? Destruction can be done so quickly; it is building or cleaning up that takes our time and energy.

On the second morning of the cleanup, I drove the kids to school, and coming back down our road, I stopped at the stop sign across from our property just as a loaded dump truck pulled out of the driveway. I turned and followed it closely. A piece of paper flew off the top of the truck and danced in the air above me. I caught my breath and slowed down, leaning forward as I tried to follow where it was going. I pulled into the driveway of our rental and jumped out. The paper was lying in the road, and I realized it was a page from a book.

But which one? I thought of my several editions of *Pride and Prejudice* and the other Austens, and the beautiful set of Barbara Pym I had collected, one by one. Could it be one of the Little House books, which I had read and reread since I was seven and treated myself to copies in hardcover when they were reissued in my thirties? I thought of the lovely edition of Elizabeth Gaskell's *Cranford* I had recently bought with the bright chartreuse cloth cover. Maybe it was a page from one of our Bibles.

Whatever, it was a rare relic of Life Before, and I had to find out what it was.

I ran out into the road, grabbed it, and rushed back to my van.

It was pages 309 and 310 of *Little Men* by Louisa May Alcott, a favorite of mine when I was a girl. On page 309, some of the boys from Jo's school are looking at a microscope with her niece Daisy and nephew Demi and her husband Mr. Bhaer. There was an illustration of the children gathered around the microscope, and the edge, the bound side, of this stray page, was burned.

I was a little disappointed. Yes, it was from a beloved book, and an especially lovely edition that had been a Christmas gift from my parents when I was nine. But I had wanted a *moment* here. I wanted it to *mean* something—to speak some kind of profound truth to our situation.

The day of the fire, I had been able to walk away from all of my possessions. But now I was clutching a scrap of paper that belonged in the trash because I finally understood what had been lost. I wanted to hold on to something—anything, even if only a piece of rubbish that remained.

But it was not the talisman I had hoped. It was just a page from a burned book.

Still, I took it with me and set it on my desk. The next day I saw it, and it occurred to me that I hadn't read both sides. I picked it up again and read page 310.

"We live in a beautiful and wonderful world, Demi, and the more you know about it the wiser and the better you will be. This little glass will give you a new set of teachers, and you may learn fine lessons from them if you will," said Mr. Bhaer, glad to see how interested the boys were in the matter.

"Could I see anybody's soul with this microscope if I looked hard?" asked Demi, who was much impressed with the power of the bit of glass.

"No, dear; it's not powerful enough for that, and never can be made so. You must wait a long while before your eyes are clear enough to see the most invisible of God's wonders. But looking at the lovely things you can see will help you to understand the lovelier things you can not see."

From the time my house was in flames, I had tried to pay attention. I thought of another talisman from the fire, a smoke-stained bookmark I had found in my desk drawer with a quote from the writer and poet Thomas Lynch: "Witness and keep track."

That was all I had tried to do, and I thought I was going to learn so much about the presence of God. In the beginning, he had felt so close, but now, months later, as the impact of our loss was finally hitting hard, he had never seemed so far away.

"What about the pug?"

I don't remember when Eden first brought it up. Life was a blur of stress and disorientation, and so I can't tell you when the Relentless Campaign, as I later came to call it, began.

"What about *what* pug?" I asked.

"The pug we're going to rescue."

Oh, that. Before the fire—seemingly a lifetime ago—I had been so eager to rescue a pug, but now, it wasn't even a question. Paul and I were in complete agreement: If—and it was an enormous if—we ever got a second dog, it wouldn't be while we were in temporary housing and struggling with all the headaches of wrangling with insurance and rebuilding. We gently explained this to Eden, and that was the end of that.

Or so we thought.

eleven

A Time to Build

Whenever we stopped by the house for the many and various meetings we had after the fire, strangers would pull over and walk up. I'm sure most had good intentions, but—just ask Paul—I've never been one for whom "it's the thought that counts" is an adequate excuse.

I'm sure it never occurred to them that what they thought was reaching out felt like trespassing to us. No one could understand how distressing it was merely having strangers cross our property line. That was bad enough, and then it was like they were following a strange script.

First the introduction: "Is this your house?" When we admitted, "Well, yes, it was," they would usually tell us where they lived.

Next came story time when our new friend would tell us about *their* traumatic experience of our fire. There were a few variations: "I was asleep when I heard the sirens; so I got up, and it looked like the woods were on fire!" or "I was on my way to work/church/golf, and when I came up over the hill and saw your house—*I couldn't believe it!*" The storyteller would usually have to stop here to reprocess the memory for a moment.

"It was a shock all right." This was what I usually said—in the beginning, when I still suffered fools politely.

One woman saw it coming. "When I saw you had had a fire, I wasn't surprised. All that chi coming down the road for years and years had to have built up." She held up both arms and made a rolling motion to demonstrate.

And then she just stared. Her eyes were that peculiar and startling blue that only tinted contacts, popular in the 1980s, could create. I knew that chi was Chinese for energy or life force, but what kind of bozo uses it in normal conversation? Not that this was anything even resembling a normal conversation.

I stared back.

We had reached the final stage: cause. Usually they had to ask, "Did they ever find out what caused it?" This time, since she already thought she knew the answer, I got right to it.

"Actually, it was arson," I said—and that was the end of that chat.

Officially the cause of our fire was declared "undetermined," but, off the record, everyone agreed it was arson. I was told arson is hard to prove, and it was just easier to say "undetermined."

Three weeks to the day after our fire, in another part of town, there was another fire that began in a garage. Four days after that, there was another, also started in a garage. Two and a half weeks after that, there was yet another, and it too began in a garage. In the news articles that followed, our house wasn't mentioned.

All the fires happened in the same area, across town from us, but following the same pattern as ours.

This is when the emails and calls began. Concerned friends sent us links to the articles. "This sounds just like your fire!" On one level, I had accepted it was arson from the very first day, but we didn't talk about it publicly for the sake of our children and in part for our own. It was so lurid, and when I talked about it, I felt tainted by the crime. It was just too much.

This was when I remembered the young man who had pulled up as we were about to cross the road on the morning of the fire. I reminded Paul, whose memory of him was vague.

"I just think it's strange he didn't offer to help us. Not everyone is a social worker [my favorite description of the EQ deficient], but it's just instinctive, almost visceral, to try to help someone who's obviously in need. It's natural to ask, 'Do you need me to call someone? Would you like to sit in my car?' Anything! And where did he *go*?"

Paul and I thought about it. We had run out of the house, saw him, ran across the road, and watched the house burn. Within minutes, the sheriff had arrived.

I looked at Paul. "He just disappeared." I tried to picture him. I knew he had dark hair and dark eyes. He was a young man, not a teenager—definitely a man, but young. He was medium-tall and drove a small to medium-size car. I thought it had four doors. That was it.

Well, one more thing that wouldn't really mean anything to most people.

"He reminded me of Joey," I told Torey. Joey was the son of my father's bookkeeper who had embezzled hundreds of thousands of dollars from the family business. Joey had worked with all of us. What a strange association!

I wrote our town's fire chief and gave my description, such as it was, and asked if there was any word on our investigation. He wrote back to say it was being handled by the sheriff's department and he had no idea if it was connected to the rash of fires in the other part of town.

The fires continued throughout the summer and into the fall—two more in August, two more in September—and then in the middle of October, I got an email: "I think they got your guy"—with a link to the news story. Eventually they posted the picture of the suspect, and as wide as my description was, he fit it.

"I can see how you thought he looked like Joey. It's kinda creepy," Torey said when she saw the picture.

He was accused of setting nine fires—the final one, he was caught in the act—but because the cause of ours was officially undetermined, it wasn't counted among them. At the arraignment, a million-dollar bond was set because he was considered a danger. He went to jail to await trial.

I was glad he was now prevented from harming others, but regarding my family's situation, I felt mostly detached. Regardless of what happened to this man who may have set our fire, nothing was going to change the fact that my home had been destroyed, my children wounded, and Paul and I were still strapped with a terrible load of stressful responsibilities. The truth is, when a crime is committed, even if the criminal is caught and "justice is served," there is never true justice for the victims; nothing is going to give them back their lives before the crime.

When the alleged arsonist was first caught, I wasn't actively angry at him. Later, when he went to trial and tried to claim no one had been hurt in the many fires he set, I would have a brief and intense explosion of rage pointed directly at him. But mostly I was angry at our situation, and I directed that anger at anyone who bugged me even the slightest.

At Eden's school there had been construction during the summer on the parking lot to try to improve the pickup and drop-off process. They added a lane to allow for at least a dozen spots to pull up and drop off your child. For many of the parents, there were really only about three spots—those closest to the door. So twenty cars could be lined up waiting, as the line inched forward, with most cars stopping closest to the door, lest their precious ones have to walk any extra steps. Every morning, when I pulled into the parking lot, my blood pressure rose. One morning, a woman parked in the drop-off lane, and everyone was in a standstill until she returned.

Before the fire, I usually chose silent hatred over open confrontation but I was beginning to see the benefits of overt aggression rather than the more passive variety. I had gotten stuck behind this woman, and when I saw her approaching, I rolled down my window to speak my mind, but the woman in the car ahead of me stole my thunder.

"What do you think you're doing? This is the DROP-OFF lane! Everyone has been backed up because they couldn't get around you! Think of someone other than yourself and park in the lot!"

The offending parker just huffed past, and catching my eye—which was certainly on her—she rolled hers, as if to say that this other wom-an—my new soul mate—had some nerve.

"She's right!" I said, sticking my head out the window. "You *shouldn't* park in the drop-off lane!" The subtext was, *You are a terrible person.* And I think she heard me loud and clear as she jumped into her car and drove away.

From then on, in the interests of preserving my sanity, I chose to park and walk Eden in to avoid the line altogether. That was an impossible dream. My car might not have been crawling through it, but I wasn't blind, and every time I walked up to the entrance, I got to see the sys-tem's dysfunction. The gym teacher, a kind and easygoing man, was out there morning and afternoon, trying to direct traffic, but many parents blithely ignored him.

"You need to thump on a few hoods," I told him. "That'll get their attention."

He laughed, but I wasn't joking.

"You give me one day and a whistle." I looked him straight in the eye. "I'll bring my own sock full of quarters."

He continued to smile, but in his eyes there was a subtle uncertainty.

After dropping Eden off that day, I walked into the office and ran into a mother I hadn't seen since the previous spring.

"I'm so sorry about your fire," she said. "How terrible! But I heard you all have had a great attitude."

"Oh . . ." I wasn't really sure what to say, since an argument could be made that our—or, at least, my—great attitude had waned, if it had every truly existed in the first place.

There were other signs to support this theory.

Reading was a great comfort, and visiting our library was a soothing return to normal life, until one day, I glanced at a glass display case showcasing a few items that were going to be available in an upcoming children's craft sale. There were the usual wares: friendship bracelets, painted rocks, barrettes, clay figurines, and Christmas ornaments. A small plaque made from a ceramic tile caught my eye. "Everything happens for a reason" was painted atop a pretty scene of rainbows and flowers. A little tag identified the artist as "Kylie, age 11."

I pictured Kylie with a blonde ponytail and a pert and freckled nose. Kylie, Kylie, Kylie. She seemed to have it all figured out. She thought things were so simple. Well, I didn't agree. Not one little bit.

If I had been on the children's library craft sale committee, I would have pulled Kylie aside and given her a little talk.

"Everything happens for a reason, Kylie? EVERYTHING? How about genocide? What's the reason for that, KYLIE? How about Hurricane Katrina, Kylie? The Bataan Death March? The Trail of Tears?"

I wanted to shove the glass case over and stomp on that plaque. Kylie and her stupid platitudes needed to be stopped.

From the very beginning, several friends and family members who knew about post-traumatic stress had been encouraging me to find a good counselor—"one trained specifically in trauma."

Trauma. Trauma. Trauma. It was like having my own personal Greek chorus. I knew they were right, and I'd been worrying about my kids from the very first day. I knew they needed support, and all three were clearly showing that the fire had taken a toll. Christopher and Lydia were at an age where it would be normal to retreat from the family somewhat, but the fire compounded everyone's need to be quiet and alone. Everyone slogged through the week, and on the weekends, we crashed. It became common for us to spend hours watching television. *At least we're together,* I told myself.

Finding a good counselor became one more seemingly impossible task. I called around to get recommendations and then called the various counselors to see if they would work with our insurance. Our entire life seemed to be caught up in saving receipts and filling out forms; I had to find someone who would bill our insurance directly—and we still had only replaced one car, so location was a consideration too. We finally found someone who met all the criteria, and then we had a family session that was a gong show.

When we arrived, Paul noticed she had done her graduate work at his alma mater and commented about the school.

"It was the worst three years of my life," she said—and that was pretty much the highlight of our time with her.

Even though that counselor didn't work out, it got me thinking. One day I asked Lydia if she ever felt scared. She didn't have to give it a thought.

"Most of the time, no, but in the morning, when I go down to take a shower, I have to pass the door to the garage, and I think about how the arsonist got into our garage, so I try not to look, but I think about how there could be someone out there and how he could do so much worse than burn our house down. So I always check."

Our rental house was a bi-level. When you walked in the front door you were on a landing with a stairway going up and another going down. The kitchen, dining room, living room, bedrooms, and one bathroom were upstairs, and downstairs was the small family room, utility room, another bathroom, and the garage. I thought the older kids would enjoy having their own bathroom and suggested they take the downstairs one. It had never occurred to me that Lydia would be afraid at all, let alone every single time she used it.

"Oh, honey! I'm sorry. Why didn't you switch to our bathroom?"

"I didn't want to disturb you and Daddy." The upstairs bathroom had one entrance off the hall and another from our bedroom. Lydia was usually the first up, and she'd get ready while the rest of us were still sleeping.

"Lydia, use the upstairs bathroom. Daddy and I want you to feel safe."

Her relief was so palpable I could have cried. What else were we missing?

Eden was experiencing anxiety of her own. I realized it with increasing concern one day when she nonchalantly told me about her safety assessment of her school, where she was in the Mandarin Immersion program. "My Chinese classroom is the safest," she said, "since it's right next to the door, and my Western classroom is second safest, since it's two doors down from the door."

It was the matter-of-fact way she said it that broke my heart.

And Christopher, well, Christopher was stirring up a flurry of emails and phone calls back and forth from school and home. When I found out Paul was going to be on a long trip overseas during conferences, I about died at the thought of facing all the teachers alone.

At Christopher and Lydia's school, the teachers sit at card tables lining the great hall, a cavernous room where the kids eat lunch. Parents can pick and choose the teachers with whom they want to meet. I made the rounds and hit Christopher's teachers first. Everyone was kind, but the general consensus was that he was having an especially terrible year. I pointed out that we all were.

"We all know about your family's trouble," one teacher told me. She didn't say "but that was so three months ago"—although the implication was there.

I wanted to point to my honor student who was struggling to get out of bed every day and to my baby who was making evacuation plans right and left. I didn't want to treat my kids like victims, *and* they were clearly still hurt. I knew this, and yet I began to feel like an excuse-making enabler until I met with their academic counselor, whom I had always liked.

I sat down and tried to talk, but I was so worn-out from all the other conferences—and everything, really—that I started to cry.

"I know what you're going through is just awful," she said with utter compassion.

I could only nod. It *was* so awful.

"Dear friends of mine had a house fire two years ago, and they had to hire an attorney and sue their insurance company. They're still in litigation."

I felt so sorry for her friends and, at the same time, profoundly grateful to talk to someone who understood.

A couple years after our fire, I read an interview with a woman who had just evacuated her home in Colorado Springs and was waiting to find out if it had burned. Years before, she had lost everything—her home and business—in another wildfire. The reporter asked if she was afraid of losing everything again, and she replied, "It's not the fear of losing stuff; it's the fear of starting over."

When I read that, I sighed hard. I knew exactly what she meant. It's almost impossible to understand the incredible and unrelenting stress a catastrophic insurance claim is unless you've been through one.

New widows and widowers are encouraged to avoid making any big financial decisions for at least a year after the death of a spouse, because everyone knows it's not a good idea to do anything with money when you aren't thinking clearly. Everyone knows this. One of the hardest aspects of a house fire is having to make thousands of decisions—from what spatula to buy to how big to build the new house—while under the influence of a scorching case of post-traumatic stress.

As if that's not enough, you get to haggle with insurance about the value of everything you lost until it feels like all your money is on thousands of plates spinning in the air.

After I did my part with the inventory—listing make, model, new, used, gift, or anything else I knew about every single one of the thousands and thousands and thousands of items that filled our home—it went back to the public adjuster who was representing us and to the content specialists hired by the insurance company. Both sides would price every item and then compare notes and negotiate.

We had replacement insurance, so I thought the adjuster and the insurance company would add up the value of all our stuff and give us a big, fat check, but that's not how it works. That's not how any of it works.

For example, I had an antique cupboard my parents gave us when Paul and I first got married. It had come from my great-grandfather's farm, and I was at least the fourth generation to use it. It was a true antique—more than a hundred years old. Insurance wanted to give us $250. You couldn't get it in an antique store for less than $500, and true replacement cost—if you had bought something from Pottery Barn or Restoration Hardware, with nowhere near the quality—would have been more than $2000.

That's just one of thousands and thousands of items that needed to be valued and haggled over. It would have been hard enough if it was just about the money but these were my memories. And it wasn't just that the antique cupboard was worth more than they were willing to pay me; it was that I remembered it in my grandfather's house and then in my own childhood home and then in my own. Eden and her cousin Ren made a little house in the lower cupboard. Now they were too big, and the cupboard was lost forever.

At the same time, I had to create an inventory addendum. I needed to list all the things that had been completely destroyed—everything in the garage and the entire second floor—*from memory*, terrified I was going to forget something or, even if I managed to remember it all, that our insurance would undervalue it.

We had decided to rebuild on the property. We first considered buying another house outright and selling the lot, but after a lot of thought and prayer and several house tours, we decided to rebuild on the same property—*our* property.

You would think the township had had enough fun putting out hoops for us to jump through, one by one, in order to tear down the old house, but no; we didn't even have the old house torn down yet when they challenged our plans for the new one.

One issue was the setbacks. The rules on how close the house could be to the property lines had changed in the sixty years since the house had been built, and the township wouldn't grandfather us in under the old guidelines. We tried to buy a little land from our neighbors, but they preferred to hold on to all their acreage.

The other issue was the mother-in-law suite. We decided to build a little apartment for my mother, who had been a widow for years, living on limited means with a disability, and she was only getting older.

I had thought we would place her apartment in the basement of the new house, but the builder strongly advised against it. He recommended we build it on the first floor behind the garage for ease of access for an aging parent. To do so would greatly increase the cost, but we saw the wisdom and agreed.

Regrettably, the township did not. When the builder presented our plans, they were rejected because they deemed our property would be a duplex—and the area wasn't zoned for duplexes. Never mind that Mom's little place was entirely separate from our house and hidden behind the garage. It was entirely invisible from the street. *So close, but no cigar*, the township said. And this is when I about lost my mind. The mother-in-law suite had to be attached to our house in order not to be considered a duplex. After a bit of back-and-forth with the architect, the builder came up with a design for an enclosed breezeway connecting the main house to Mom's little cottage. This would be even more expensive, but it seemed to be the only solution. He presented it at a second township meeting at which we were also requesting a variance on the setbacks. Even though we moved the house and planned to excavate a portion of a hill to make room for it, we still didn't meet the current restrictions.

Paul was on another trip overseas, but I brought all the kids and my mother to the meeting, where we sat all in a row while our request was discussed. If the board was going to reject our plan, they would have to do it right to our faces. One of our kind neighbors came along and spoke on our behalf, and the architect did a great job presenting the challenges of the project, as well as the ordeal we had already endured. The plans and the variance were unanimously approved.

We broke ground on January 25, Eden's eighth birthday—almost seven months to the day after the fire and so much later than we had hoped. When I learned groundbreaking would be on Eden's birthday, I thought it would be meaningful. The day they tore the house down, I have a picture of her posing in front of the pile of rubble, making double peace signs with a huge eye-crinkling, open smile.

"It's so beautiful!" she said more than once when we drove by on the way to school. She was able to look past the ruins and see the hills and the trees that had sheltered us and now were all that was left. I assumed the day we broke ground would be an even happier one.

For her birthday, Paul and I gave her a pair of Chinese hamsters—which (in addition to a pug) she had been begging for. Up until then, we had maintained a "no rodents as pets" policy, but desperate times call for desperate measures, and I was trying to be strategic.

Despite sitting down with Eden and gently explaining that *if* we ever adopted another dog—and that was an enormous if—there was no way we'd do it while living in a rental and trying to rebuild, none of that mattered to Eden, and it did nothing to diminish her obsession with rescuing a pug.

"I will do all the work!" was her favorite plea. "I feed Jack every day!"

"There is more to dog ownership than mere feeding," Paul countered. "What about the expense? Who buys the food? Who pays Jack's vet bills?"

"I'll earn the money for the pug!"

"It's so much more than just buying the dog. It's a lifetime of food and vet bills. What if it had a health problem? Would you be able to pay for that?" Paul tried to reason with her.

We had these conversations every couple of weeks. "What if we got her the hamsters for her birthday? Maybe she'll forget about the pug," I suggested to Paul privately.

On her birthday, we gave her a little cage and all the supplies she would need for her hamsters, which we told her she could pick out the next day. She was delighted. Old family friends were in town, and we had a nice little dinner party. After cake and ice cream, we all walked down to check out the excavation. None of us had seen it yet. When the site came into view, we were too shocked to speak. The entire landscape had changed.

Eden's garden, which had survived the fire, and most of the hill to the west of our property were gone. I knew we were repositioning the house, but it hadn't yet quite registered what this would mean. I vaguely knew we would be losing part of the hill, but I couldn't have imagined it'd be so much of it. I felt sideswiped.

Even after the fire and the demolition, our property was still so beautiful, but now it looked ravaged. It was January, a savage-feeling time anyway—and on that day, there was no layer of snow to soften and cover the landscape. Everything looked torn apart and raw.

The first shock wore off, and we wandered around. Our friend, who is a carpenter and accustomed to building sites, discussed the details of the house with Paul. I, who had planned every inch of the house and was already sick and tired of it, walked over to Eden, who was standing alone, a safe distance from the hole.

"My garden is gone," she whispered.

"I know, honey. I'm so sorry."

"I was so happy it made it through the fire. I thought it was safe." She started to cry.

"I'm so sorry. I didn't think. I knew we were moving the house, but I just didn't think about your garden. I'm so, so sorry." I was crying too.

We'd lost the house, and I thought that was the worst of it. But I was wrong. The losses—little and large—kept coming in waves. And after losing so much, it's incredibly painful to lose anything you had counted as safe.

❧   ❧   ❧

Once we broke ground, I had so many decisions to make. Building a house requires making hundreds of decisions—and you have to make them in a timely fashion or you'll mess up the schedule. This is stressful and overwhelming for homeowners with planned builds; for me, addled by exhaustion, it was excruciating. I had to force myself to do what needed to be done, and it's not like I could set down the rest of the plates I already had spinning.

While shopping for appliances, I got a call from Eden's school counselor. Eden had been meeting with her that year and in their most recent time together had said how anxious she felt. I leaned against a kitchen display and quietly discussed strategies to support my worried and overwhelmed girl.

"Building a house is soooooo stressful. You have so many decisions to make. It's so hard," the salesman said when I returned. He knew our house had burned down and that I had excused myself to talk to my child's counselor, but these little details were lost on him.

A couple of weeks later, when I was shopping for tile, my phone rang again. I saw that it was Christopher's school and felt a pang in my chest. Experience had taught me that this probably wasn't going to be good. I excused myself from the saleswoman and walked toward the entrance.

It was Christopher's support teacher asking me to come to school to pick him up. He had brought a weapon to school and was being suspended.

WHAT!

It was his small Swiss Army knife. The teacher knew Christopher well and didn't think he intended to harm anyone, but she was required to take the knife away and report it. When she asked him why he brought it to school, he said, "It makes me feel safe." And the entire antibullying protocol swung into action. There would be a mandatory three-day suspension while the school investigated and made sure no one was bullying him. I wanted to put my head down and cry, but I didn't have time.

I apologized to the tile saleswoman and headed for the car, calling Paul as I walked. By some miracle, he was able to get away, and I drove straight to his office to pick him up. On the way we talked. Neither of us could believe Christopher had consciously taken a "weapon" to school. He loved his knife. He was constantly whittling things or whipping it out in emergencies, especially after the fire when we had no other tools. Several times, Christopher and his Swiss Army knife had saved the day. We were almost positive he had simply forgotten or maybe didn't even know he wasn't supposed to take it to school. But how could we demonstrate that? And why did he say it made him feel safe?

"We have to remember it's one of the only things he was able to save after the fire. I wonder if making him feel safe has to do with providing a basic sense of security and not from it being a means of defense," Paul said.

I hadn't considered that, but it made total sense. At the school, we met with Christopher, his teacher, and the vice principal. Christopher's eyes were red and wide. "I'm so sorry," he said. He was clearly scared. Paul and I both hugged him.

"Would you ask him *why* the knife made him feel safe?" I asked the teacher, and she did.

Christopher answered without a moment's hesitation. "Because it's one of my only possessions." His voice broke, and tears shot out of his eyes. He winked them away. "And it was a gift from my grandmother."

The adults all exchanged glances. Christopher's teacher escorted him to his locker to get his backpack while Paul and I spoke privately with the vice principal. He didn't think Christopher was a threat and was fairly certain he wasn't being threatened, but the three-day suspension was mandatory while they investigated. Just as we all suspected, there was nothing to discover, and at the end of three days, Christopher returned to school, but this wouldn't be the last call I received from them, not by a long shot.

Meanwhile, the pug lover didn't let up. The hamster operation was a flop. "I thought they would be cuddly! They aren't at all cuddly!" It had done nothing to stop The Relentless Campaign.

"I'll earn the money for the pug!" was Eden's constant cry. Finally, in a moment of utter weariness and weakness, Paul agreed she could start saving money, *but*—he made it clear—this was not a commitment. If she wanted to work and earn the money while we lived in the rental, she could do that, and at the end of the day, *if* we still weren't ready for another dog, she would have hundreds of dollars to save or spend as she pleased. Key words here being *but* and *if.*

Eden agreed and began to work like—well, like a dog. At the old house, we had taught Jack to do his business in the woods, but in the rental, we only had an aerial run—basically a leash attached to a clothesline—and the yard was a mess. One Saturday, Eden saw Paul shoveling pile after pile. When Eden asked if she could help, Paul hired her on the spot. She already fed and watered Jack morning and night, for which she was paid a small amount. She made flyers to send to family and friends:

I am starting a Bissnes.
Pet care and gardening
and I want to know if you need any help!
Love, Eden

There was no job too hard or too lowly for her, and the money started to add up. Before we knew it, Eden's Pug Fund was in full force. Within weeks, she had more than a hundred dollars, and counting. Working for her pug became a bright and cheerful spot in an otherwise dark time. She began to keep a journal of sorts. I saw her writing in it frequently. It was a simple spiral notebook with a picture of a fawn pug puppy on the cover. "Pug List," Eden had written in her sprawling hand, and she drew a little heart beneath it. Years later, she told me she named it this because she didn't know how to spell *diary*. Back then, I didn't even wonder what it was. She was always composing poems or songs or writing stories, so I didn't give it a second thought. I was just happy she was a little bit happier.

Paul and I were too busy to think about what would happen if she were to save all the money and we still didn't want another dog. We could worry about that another day. At least as far as thinking about a pug went, today had more than enough trouble of its own.

One of the very last things I had to select for the new house was doors and hardware.

"I've heard that building a house is the biggest stress on a marriage," the salesman said, and I was astonished. We had just had an extensive conversation about the awfulness of fires. He was even friends with a man whose son had died in one.

Maybe he was trying to sympathize, but I didn't feel it, so Debbie Downer: Fire Lady Edition replied, "I've found that someone burning my house down before I rebuilt it to be more stressful still." He nodded, cheerfully oblivious, and asked if I wanted locks on all the bedroom doors.

At the old house, only Lydia had a lock on her door. It wasn't planned—it just happened to be her room—but to Eden and Christopher, it had always seemed an injustice. I thought about how happy they would be to finally have locks on their doors too.

"Yes, all the bedrooms," I said, and then I remembered smacking Christopher to wake him up to get him out of the house. I imagined the new house on fire—and Christopher locked in his room, sleeping and unable to hear—and I burst into tears. I tried to explain between sobs and stopped myself short of apologizing.

The salesman did it for me. "I'm so sorry," he said, which is really the only thing you should say, and I thanked him.

As the house neared completion, people began to ask, "Are you at the fun stage yet?" The first time, I had no idea what the questioner meant. In this case, she was a lovely person, a mother of one of Eden's classmates, whose parents had been through a house fire themselves. Her mother, who wasn't in the house at the time of the fire and whose children were grown, really enjoyed buying new furniture. To outsiders, the idea of being given a huge pile of cash to buy all new things was tantalizing. If only that's how it really worked. Since our insurance was fighting us tooth and nail and briefly accused us of fraud—so, no, we hadn't actually been given the huge pile of cash—the fun stage had so far eluded us. But the question remained in the back of my head as the stress-filled and miserable months passed. I wasn't enjoying any bit of our house fire and felt like a failure. I was beleaguered by the thought of other, better, stronger, more upbeat women who would be able to fully appreciate the benefits of a fire. Alas, I wasn't one of them. This was a serious regret—until it finally occurred to me, much further down the road, there may not be a fun stage to arson.

twelve

Home Again, but Not

We didn't so much move back into the new house as we were coughed up into it. That's how it felt. It was strange to think of being back in a place that's entirely new. We expected it to feel like a homecoming, but it didn't feel like home.

"Oh, you'll put your stamp on it," a friend said.

She was right—we would. The thing about losing almost all your possessions is that, temporarily anyway, your stamp is taken away. I said again and again losing our belongings was not the source of suffering after our fire, and we all know, in theory at least, that stuff is only stuff, and yet possessions do have emotional value. There is great comfort in the familiarity of things owned for many years. It was only after we moved into our new house that I realized I had been in a bubble of transition and waiting, expecting closure where I couldn't possibly find it. I had thought that moving into the new house would feel like coming home from a long trip. But it didn't.

A couple weeks after we moved in, Paul and I were walking with Eden, and she started to cry.

"I don't like the new house. It's so clean and perfect, and there's almost nothing in it. I want our wonky old house. I found something new there every day! Why did you have to change it? Why couldn't you build it just like the old one?"

I had spent years trying to make the old house beautiful, working slowly from the inside out. It was finally beginning to look charming, cottage-like, in the way I had imagined when we first bought it.

I wanted the new house to look like a traditional white farmhouse, and the architect designed it with clean and simple lines. It is much nicer than the old one, solidly built, with hardwood floors, beautiful cabinetry, soapstone countertops, well-proportioned rooms, and so many windows that it's always filled with light. And yet I knew exactly what Eden meant.

But then she went on. "And I don't like our family now! We use bad words, and we never listen to music anymore, like when we used to dance in the living room!"

She was like my pint-sized subconscious, saying out loud all the things I was silently bemoaning, giving voice to all my regrets. I had been trying to talk myself out of these very complaints. The house was beautiful; we were fortunate to have a home at all, and I should be grateful. I had my priorities straight in the beginning. How had I lost perspective? None of this helped and having Eden right there, reinforcing all of it, made everything even more difficult. I had spent too much money. I was sure I had made so many mistakes.

Christopher and Lydia were less outspoken. Both said they liked the new house . . . and it wasn't home.

The house was supposed to be the happy ending to our story. That's what everyone had said over and over. "At least you get a beautiful new house!" It was simple math: house fire + brand-new house = worth it! Happily ever after! But the story wasn't over—not for us—and in some ways, it was only beginning.

When we moved back, we faced the fact that a crime had been committed. The fire didn't just happen; it had been set.

"I just don't understand why he did it," Eden would say. How do you help a child understand what you don't understand yourself, what is incomprehensible? Though I had dealt with the effects, every single day since the fire, I still couldn't really believe someone started it. I hated the fact that my children lived in a world where someone can burn your house down, and I couldn't remove that sorrow. It haunted us all.

After we decided to rebuild on the site, I was asked more than once, "Are you nervous about moving back?" I said I didn't think I was—yet.

Which is so strange, since I had spent most of my life anxious and worried, and it was in that house—the one a madman would burn down—that I finally surrendered fear.

My earliest memories are of being afraid, of not feeling safe at night.

I didn't understand the people who said ridiculous things like, "There's nothing to be afraid of." Didn't they watch the news?

After Paul and I had gotten married, whenever he traveled, I was always scared. I couldn't sleep, and I prayed incessantly, asking God to take away my fear. I thought of 1 John 4:18 (NKJV): "Perfect love casts out fear."

"I guess I don't have enough love," I had said and then asked him to take away the fear.

After we had closed on our house but before we moved in, I noticed there was a security system. *Why would a house that doesn't have a dishwasher have an alarm system?* I wondered but pushed the thought from my mind. This was fine until a couple days before we moved in, the neighbor two houses down came home and found a man with panty hose over his face in her kitchen. He ran out the back door and over the hill that cradled all our homes. It was the middle of the day.

My next-door neighbor told Paul, "We've never had any trouble, but your place was broken into several years ago." Hence the alarm. When Paul told me about the break-in, I was stunned.

"When we move in, we're going to activate the alarm," he told me firmly, trying to stave off the panic he knew was mounting. Too late. It confirmed my supposition that there is no safe place. A friend who lived in a crime-ridden neighborhood couldn't understand. "You live in such a safe part of town."

Years before, I had written in a journal (that would eventually burn) the words of Betsie ten Boom, whose family famously worked in the Dutch resistance and hid Jews in Nazi-occupied Netherlands. Her sister, Corrie, lived to tell the story, but Betsie and several other family members died in prison and concentration camps.

In Corrie's beloved book *The Hiding Place*, she tells of how being led to join Betsie in the kitchen had protected her from being struck by a shard of shrapnel that fell onto her pillow in her bedroom during a night of bombings. In response to Corrie's "if I hadn't heard you in the kitchen . . . ," Betsie said, "There are no 'ifs' in God's world. And no places that are safer than other places. The center of His will is our only safety—Oh Corrie, let us pray that we may always know it!"

This quote resonated with me, and I wrote it down, though I completely missed the point. Since the only safe place is with God, who transcends time and space, it should be possible to live fearlessly anywhere. I knew this was the point of it, but I lived in this statement alone: There is no safe place.

We had moved into that house and activated the alarm, and when Paul was out of town, I religiously set it at night and whenever we left the house. And it helped. When I woke up in the wee hours and *knew* that someone was in the house, I reminded myself, even though I had left the back door unlocked all day while I was out, I had set the alarm so no one had slipped in and was now lying in wait in the attic. It helped unravel my irrational tangle of fears.

At the same time, things were shifting for me spiritually. I had been raised in the church and "asked Jesus into my heart" (as some of us say) when I was five, but I had never really felt God's love. He had shown up for me profoundly, even miraculously, and in some ways, I trusted him deeply, but somehow I had missed that sense of an abiding, overarching, and tender love. Yet that was changing. I began to feel God's love so deeply and was swept over by his care of me.

I read the Bible, which I had done since I was able to read, and was shocked. "The Bible is *full* of God's love!" I told people, clutching at their sleeves. Nobody actually said, "Um, duh!" but it was implied. I didn't care; I was dazzled by the light of God's grace and his love, and one day, I realized I wasn't afraid anymore. I still had fears, but fear itself was not the undercurrent of everything.

It occurred to me that I had spent so many years asking for God to remove my fears when I should have been asking him to fill me with his love. I'm not saying it's like voodoo, that I didn't say the right incantation. It isn't like that. But clearly I was focusing on the wrong part of the equation. If perfect love casts out fear—I knew this intellectually, if not practically—then love is the handle I ought to be grabbing. Why? "Because," the apostle John goes on to declare, "fear involves torment"— and ain't that the truth! "But he who fears has not been made perfect in love. We love Him because He first loved us" (1 John 4:18–19 NKJV).

So the house in which I learned to set aside fear gets set on fire, and when I'm asked if I'm scared to move back, I'm not sure. I figured there would be some sort of an adjustment, but when we were rebuilding, I knew that was tomorrow's worry, and "today" so clearly had enough worries of its own. First I was worried my kids would be scarred forever; then I was worried the township would never let us tear down the ruins; then that they would never approve the new plans; then that insurance would never pay; then that the new house was going to be a billion dollars and the kids would be eating ketchup soup and never be able to go to college. But was I worried about our physical safety? Not so much. I figured that lesson had been learned.

Then a couple months before we moved, I dreamed someone was breaking into the house. Paul held the door of the room we were locked in while I called 911. I woke up in a panic. It was clear, consciously or not, that I was anxious as we prepared to return and make our home at the scene of the crime.

One morning, a few weeks after we moved back, I awoke early, at not quite five o'clock. We still hadn't bought clocks and my phone was in the kitchen, so I went downstairs to get a drink of water and check the time. I noticed it was just a little later than it had been the morning of the fire. Other than in the earliest days, or briefly after they caught him, I hadn't given much thought to the architect of the entire situation. But I did think of him that morning as I walked back upstairs and peeked out one of the windows in the hall. I wondered if he had crept across the lawn. I scanned the yard, pausing where the trees cast deeper shadows.

Behind me, their bedrooms all in a row, the children slept. I went into each room, one by one, and prayed over my son and daughters. Lydia stirred as I kissed her but didn't fully wake. My niece Ren was having a sleepover with Eden. Their heads were so close that their hair tangled together. I pushed back their hair to lay my hands on their warm foreheads. Christopher was sleeping deeply and never knew I was there. I got back into my own bed to try to go back to sleep.

I had barely snuggled in when our security alarms began to whoop. Paul and I jumped to our feet. He stopped at the security panel by our bedroom door, and I ran down the hall. Eden and Ren met me. I put an arm around each one of them and pulled them close.

"We're OK," I told them. Lydia came out of her room. "We need to get Christopher."

We got him up and hurried downstairs. I was ready to go outside, but there wasn't even a hint of smoke—we knew what to look for—so we lined up on the couch, and I tried to reach across so my arms were around all of them.

By then, Paul had stopped the alarms and was on the phone with the security company, walking through the house to ensure that everything was secure. We were safe, but Eden's heart was beating like a rabbit's.

It was only 5:15. Christopher was barely awake and went right back to bed. Paul was close behind, but he climbed into Lydia's bed so all three girls could get into our big bed with me. We were wide-awake, and the girls were shaken. I read aloud the last few chapters of *One Hundred Dresses*, a beautiful book about bullying, conviction, and forgiveness, and we all huddled together.

Later in the week, a technician from the security company came and quickly corrected the problem. Something that had never been wired properly. So it was easily taken care of, but what about us? When would we stop bolting at actual and perceived alarms?

We live at a crossroads, and although we are by two (sort of) country roads, they're busy ones. We considered adding a circle drive to the new house.

"You don't want that," a friend said. "You'll have so many cars pulling in to turn around that it'll be like the Indianapolis 500."

We changed our mind on the circle, but our new driveway was large, and drivers still used it freely.

This didn't work for me.

The first time someone pulled in, I shot out the front door. The middle-aged woman who had already turned around and was heading back out saw me and waved. I kept coming. She stopped and rolled down her window.

"I'm just turning around." She smiled, blithely unaware that she was trespassing.

"This doesn't work for me," I said, leaning close to her open window.

"Well, I'm sorry," she said with slight aggravation, as if she wasn't the one VIOLATING THE SANCTITY OF OUR PROPERTY, as if *I* was the one with a problem!

Some people just wanted a closer look at the new house. I promptly and fiercely dispatched them every time—unless Paul got there first. He is six foot six and has a way of making himself even bigger.

"Is there something I can help you with?" was his line, which I thought gave a false sense of friendliness. I preferred the less ambiguous "this doesn't work for me." I have always thought a good offense is the best defense, and it had the added benefit of complete honesty. *So much* wasn't working for me. At all.

I had tried to find another therapist with no luck, and then, while selecting flooring, the salesperson recommended one who specialized in trauma. The fact that I was getting therapist recommendations while checking out hardwood was just another confirmation of how much I needed it.

"She changed my life."

I called the therapist and scheduled all three kids for appointments. One appointment was often all children needed. With all three, we saw almost overnight results. It was incredible.

For adults, she had devised a seven-part, three-hour program, a session that had been highly successful with many clients. I met with her week after week and dutifully did all the exercises, but my anxiety only increased. By the sixth appointment, I was clearly letting her down.

"By now, I'm usually hearing rave reviews."

I already felt like such a failure. I never thought the fire was some great spiritual test, but I felt like I had flunked it all the same. It had started out so great, or at least my response to it had been so good—calm and serene—but that was quickly taken over by anxiety and rage. I had gone from the brave and saintly Fire Lady to the too-often unhinged harridan. I thought I was going to be able to get through the fire by mourning it all, but that wasn't enough. I felt like I had let God down—and everyone around me as well. I had let *myself* down. I had proven to be so much less than I thought I could be. And now, apparently, I was even failing therapy.

❧   ❧   ❧

I was prone to waking in the night before the fire, and in the new house, I conducted a night patrol. Whenever I woke up, without even thinking, I went to one of the north-facing windows. It was frequently the one in our bathroom or one of the three in the hall outside our bedrooms; sometimes, but rarely, it was the one in the laundry room, and if I ever went down to the kitchen, I always peered out the one at the bottom of the stairs. The morning of the false alarm was the first time I did it, and from then on, I subconsciously made it a practice. I was looking for the arsonist—or rather, his absence. I was checking to make sure he wasn't there.

It was habitual and even subconscious—I was just assessing conditions. My eyes went first to the two spruces on the east side of our driveway, near the maple we had briefly gathered under the morning of the fire before running across the road and watching the house burn, the trees backlit by flames.

Often my eyes would scan to the other side of the drive, where the hill slopes down to the redbud and the three new and larger spruces, looking to see the arsonist creeping toward the house, or to make sure he wasn't.

A vapor light on the corner illuminates the two trees and the front lawn, but the other side is mostly in shadow. I would scan it all before I made the subconscious call that would free me to go back to sleep: no arsonist, not today.

It took months of living in the house to understand why I was doing this.

It was a strange vigilance. I didn't consciously reason that if I keep a close watch, this time I won't be caught off guard—if he is out there, this time he isn't going to get us.

I continued to wonder where he had walked—if he strode up the drive or crept along the edge of the woods in nearly total darkness. Where had he parked his car? It was like this itch in my brain I just couldn't scratch. I really wanted to know. It took me years to see the reason for my fixation. I guess I thought if I knew the details of how he did it, I could finally accept that he did, and maybe even begin to understand why.

thirteen

The Pug List

One day I walked in on Eden lying in bed, her eyes closed, arms stretched out, palms up.

"Just a second, Mom," she said. "I'm praying."

"OK."

"I'm asking God if our house is going to burn down again."

Oh, that hurt.

"Only he knows," she said, as if it was the most natural thing in the world—and it is—and then she shut her eyes again. I perched beside her and waited.

After a minute or so, her blue eyes opened, and we looked at each other. I may have been holding my breath.

"I think he said no."

"I think you're right," I said.

She might have hated our new, shiny, clean house, but she didn't want to lose it. It was complicated—but through it all, one thing brought her unstoppable joy: the possibility of a pug.

I had hoped that in the excitement and busyness of the move Eden would forget about the Relentless Campaign. I thought, like so many other childish enthusiasms, it would fade in time. But she didn't forget. It didn't fade. And she didn't give up.

That fall, we had the estate sale for my mother, whom we had moved into her new little apartment when we moved back. I titled the Craigslist ad "If Martha Stewart Was a Hoarder"—and sure enough, it drew a crowd.

For months, Eden had been collecting things to sell, including expensive Christmas and birthday presents. When I remonstrated, she didn't back down. "Mama, I'm earning money for the pug. I want the pug more than I want the stuff!"

At the sale, she set up a little table on the front porch and did brisk business. An elderly couple, buying for their granddaughter, tried to haggle her down to less than pennies on the dollar. When I tried to step in, Eden waved me aside.

"It's for the pug!"

I gave the old man the stink eye, and he added a couple dollars to the price.

Others were far more generous. When they heard what she was saving for, several gave extra as a donation.

Soon, word about Eden's campaign got around. One night, a family friend came over for dinner. He had received Eden's flyer but was traveling too much to have her come over to do some yard work. He pulled out a $50 bill and gave it to Eden.

"That's for your Pug Fund," he said. Eden's face lit up.

"Thank you so much!" She remembered her manners before hustling upstairs to add it to the pile.

She already had almost $300 saved. There were a few rescues that accepted less than that, but the standard fee was $350. She was getting so close and was starting to get excited. Meanwhile, Paul and I were getting nervous. What were we going to do when she had enough?

I expressed my concerns to him one morning while he was getting dressed. He turned away from the closet and looked at me. "To be honest, I'm weakening." A cold horror rushed over me.

"What do you mean?" I asked.

"About the pug."

I gasped. "You have *got* to be kidding me!" Paul was the level-headed one. I was counting on *him*!

He looked sheepish. "My little girl has been working so long and so hard, and I don't know how I can't reward that."

I couldn't believe it. I was the one who'd had an online romance—as passionate as it was impractical—with Tonka when Paul was advocating against a second dog. He didn't even *like* pugs.

I would always love pugs, but I decided I was happy to limit my admiration to the ones I met at the park or online. The memory of my love for Tonka had faded. I realized in missing out on him, we had dodged a bullet. For me, a pug had been reduced to just one more thing that sheds—in a shade different from Jack's. Thank you, no.

I am not a fastidious woman, and yet Jack's fur had been my life's bane for four years. I knew he would be a terrible shedder, but like so many things, to know something intellectually is a world apart from experiencing it. To know your dog is a shedder is one thing, and then to actually sweep three times a day and still be able to do "snow angels" in the dog hair is another.

Black dog hair naturally shows up against anything that is lighter, which is . . . everything. When we leave the house, we float in a cloud of black fur, but it's not sticking to our clothes; we just sort of carry it with us. But most pugs are fawn, which means their fur shows up against anything darker—that's pretty much everything too.

I could already see every light and dark surface in our new house perpetually ruined. I was already losing my one-woman fight against fur in our new, entirely white house. I swept and vacuumed and dusted more in those first five months than I had in the previous five years, and I was still losing my mind.

Now that Paul had gone rogue, I was nervous. This was a complete role reversal. I was always the one pulling for something, and Paul the one who resisted: Tonka, Jack, even Eden herself. Paul thought we had our hands full with two children and wasn't sure a third was the best idea, but I knew our family wasn't complete. Every time, he finally came around, but only after long delays for all of them. Now here he was, folding like a card table. This shouldn't have surprised me. Despite any initial resistance, it was always Paul who surrendered to his family, to love.

I just kept hoping Eden's passion would slowly melt away, but instead it kept growing. But then again, nothing had been the way I thought. I thought we were *fine*. I thought we had what it took to sail through the aftereffects of the fire with all our flags flying. Who would have believed that now, more than a year after the fire, months after moving into the new house, I would still feel so incredibly wrecked? And yet things can change so quickly—I certainly knew that—but that's the whole problem: You can't see the curve balls until they're about to hit you in the face.

One day when I was looking for something in her room, I came across her little notebook, her "Pug List." When I picked it up, it fell open, and I couldn't resist a peek.

Inside the front cover, she wrote:

To: the good pug I WiLL
Have!
I Thing I Think That my
Pug List is so FUU
FUnnnnnnnnnnnnnnnnnnnnnnn!!!

Her first entry:

Dear Pug LiST, I almosT
Have a Enough mony
For a pug. But my
parats say NO! and
I. Do Not Like it one
Bit. But I try and try to
get Enough mony!
But it is a hard thing
To do. But it is
Wothe it. But the Th
pug motivates me. ad
and it makes me HAPPY!
so I Just keep
working and working
all Day Long! the
pugs make me
Happy FOREVER.

I read this and felt the first sense of foreboding and shut the book, but later I had to take another look. On the facing page was a large heart on the top of the page, and then a one-sentence question written so large that it took up its entirety:

Why
is a
pug
so goo-
d ???

I read on:

yay! I Have so much
mony! I Have 113$ and
someThing cenTs! and I
am so Excited! and
my goal is To Have
Enough mony By The
Time my hoes is BiuL
BulT. So Then I can
may get a pug! and
For a Thing To happen!
sh my sisten wants me to hurry up so . . .
good bye
pug LisT!!

The house was certainly "BulT"—but still no pug.

well Hello pug List,
It is so Fun Trying to get a pug. I Eden
Hodgson, Will get a pug
and I am so Happy
about it! What
can make a gir girl
happyer then a pug?
Huh?? I love pugs so
MUCH Yes I Do and someDay I
will Have
one oF my oun. I ♡ pugs.
[With a curving arrow down to a drawing of a pug on
the bottom of the page.]

When had she become a world-class motivational writer? This was
the stuff that would make Zig Ziglar or Joel Osteen envious. But she was
just getting started.

Dear a Pug List,
I Have $115.12! I am Haveing
such a fun time with
pug List. and c NoBody can change

That ♡

[she artfully centered the exclamation point
over the heart]
the Deal is to Not
stop trying hard Eouth. then it
makes it funer.
I Love pugs

This is when I might have said one of those "bad words" Eden didn't like us saying.

Once Paul and I agreed that Eden could earn the money for the pug, we sort of tuned out all the pug talk. It became a low-level yammering in the background, getting in line behind other more pressing issues— and there were so many. A pug was "tomorrow's worry." I think I was just relieved to have Eden's ardent desire redirected away from pressure and persuasion and focused on earning. I had known it was going on, but the seeming letup gave me a false sense of relief. It was clear we had been leading her on and giving her a false sense of hope. In our defense, we had made it clear there was no commitment. We had played fair. We weren't letting her down. We had never promised her anything.

But as I read her precious Pug List, I realized this airtight reasoning fell completely flat. We had approached the whole business with our heads: "Why don't you work and earn the money, and then we'll see. No promises." If there had been a contract, we weren't breaking it. She didn't have a thing on us legally. But you can't think in legal terms when it's your kid's heart on the line. Because I had finally gotten this message as clearly as the symbol she had scrawled on the cover of her Pug List: This was about my little girl's heart.

I think we all have those moments that shine out from our child-hoods, when something was so important, and maybe our parents meant no harm, but they let us down anyway, and it hurt so much.

Somewhere down the road, Eden was going to learn that you can work and work, try your hardest, and give it your all—and you still won't get what you want. That's just life. But did I want her to learn that at my hands? No.

And I really, really, really didn't want another dog.

fourteen

Rescue Me

After I read Eden's Pug List I knew we had a problem. And I was completely clear I had no idea how we were going to solve it, so I did the only thing I know to do when I don't know what to do: I prayed. Eden's sweet hope and optimism kept replaying in my mind.

> Dear Pug List . . .
> I LOVE trying to get a
> pug. So much! I Have so
> Much money I can't
> Even Imagine How
> Much I Have!!!!!

> Dear Pug List,
> I am sooooo happy

Dear Pug List, Dear Pug List, Dear Pug List! What were we going to do?

The answer didn't come immediately. For a few weeks, I was still tight and apprehensive, until one day, something occurred to me. When I mentioned it to Paul, he gave his blessing.

"What would you think about looking for a black pug?" I asked Eden.

Black pugs are much less common than fawns. In the year I stalked Tonka, there had only been one or two black pugs in the statewide pug rescue network. This might have occurred to me when I made Eden my offer. Regardless, it was the bridge that carried us over. Eden accepted without a moment's hesitation.

"Yes," she said, her eyes shining, "it's a great idea. Yes."

We hit Petfinder immediately but there were no black pugs. We saw plenty of adorable fawns, but none of them stole our hearts like Tonka had.

After a few weeks of searching, a snapshot of a little black pug named Jet popped up from a rescue across the state. Eden and I both gasped, and I clicked on the profile.

Jet was a three-year-old male with—even for a pug—wide, bulging eyes. His profile said he was friendly and well-behaved and, most important of all, housebroken. I leaned forward to study him, clicking back and forth, enlarging the two pictures. He looked worried, almost frightened, but he was cute. He was so cute.

"What do you think?" I asked Eden.

"Yes," she said, without a moment's hesitation.

"You want to check him out?"

"Yes!"

I knew the next step was to fill out the application, so I followed the link and downloaded the form. Right away, I was impressed with its size—an issue they addressed at the top of the first page.

Note: The purpose of this application is not to make adopting a pug difficult but to ensure that the right person is chosen for the right pug. Since these animals have already experienced a traumatic situation when they lost their previous home, we feel strongly about being completely thorough with our applicants. Thank you for your understanding.

Extensive paperwork overwhelms me in the best of times, and I had just spent a year filling out enough forms to last a lifetime, but I understood traumatic situations and displacement, and I certainly wanted the right pug. I set to work with Eden by my side. It began with "Personal Information": name, address, length of time at the address, current employer, and three personal references not related to or living with the applicant. And they wanted the name, age, and gender of every member of the household. This was definitely going to be thorough.

Are you expecting a child or planning a family in the near future? While this question could qualify as prying, I understood it. How many times had I heard about a couple surrendering an animal after having a baby because they "could no longer devote the necessary time, and it was not fair" to the animal?

Next was "Environmental Information." They wanted to know everything—and I do mean everything—about our house, down to whether we had stairs, and did they have open backs and where were they located. This I understood too—my own kids, after all, liked to keep tabs on their exit plan.

I continued answering question after question regarding our "Pet History" (with Jack) and "Behavior" questions about what we were hoping for in a pug.

"Veterinarian Information" was next.

What would your yearly health care budget be for your pug? I wasn't sure what to say. There was a list of suggested expenses, which included immunizations, heartworm testing, emergency care, and routine checkups. I noticed there was no mention of gastric lavage, something I now counted under general dog care and felt smug about. I was clearly an expert dog owner by now.

What will you do if your pug has a major illness or injury and the cost exceeds your budget? "It depends" probably wouldn't cut it, but we hadn't set aside a certain amount. Given Jack's history, we knew what was possible but didn't really want to think about it. "I would steal from home maintenance" was the most honest answer but I wrote, "We have a general emergency fund for unexpected expenses." They wanted to know if our vet was familiar with pugs and all their contact information as well as if we had access to an emergency vet and if they were open 24/7. Oh yes. I made a little note to get the addresses for both.

Then came "Pug Knowledge and Care."

Are you aware of health problems that a pug may have? God help me, I was. *If yes, what problems do you foresee? Please explain.* I said I knew about their breathing problems, how they easily became overheated, how their buggy eyes were vulnerable, how their teeth were crap—why did we want a pug again? Oh, yes, it was this eager and insistent little person beside me. I carried on page after page, question after question, answering each one with care, and yet I felt confident. I knew we were good applicants.

When I was sure I had filled out the entire application, I gathered everything, wrote the check for the application fee, and had Eden run it out to the mailbox. I carefully composed an email to the rescue director to express interest and inform him that the application was on its way. I tried to be as straightforward as possible. There was no need to tell our life story—the application had already pretty much done that for me. I hit Send and was surprised to realize I was excited.

I called our vet's office, and the kindly office manager agreed to print off Jack's file and send it to the rescue that day. She offered to write a quick reference and mailed me a copy, which arrived the next day.

Dear Rescue Members,

Re: Pet Owners Alison and Paul Hodgson

Please accept this letter of reference on behalf of Alison and Paul Hodgson. I understand that they are wishing to adopt a pug from your organization. I could not think of a more loving and responsible family for you to place a pet in. As you can see from Jack's extensive history, they have gone above and beyond to provide Jack with the best medical care. They are very trustworthy pet owners and always make a concerted effort to ensure that Jack is happy and healthy.

Please do not hesitate to call me if I can be of additional assistance.

Handwritten on the letter was a smiley face with this note: "We FedExed Jack's history (18 pages!)."

I smiled too. Like they said—*above and beyond*. After all my years of hard work, caring for and training Jack, after years of longing to be a good dog owner, it was wonderful to see all of it acknowledged.

The meet and greet was scheduled for the next Saturday, and Eden's little heart was bursting with joy and excitement.

Of course, by now, I should have known that nothing ever goes as planned. The day after we sent the letter—just to spite us, it seemed—Eden fell and broke her arm. The week became a blur of doctor appointments.

And then, Paul's aunt died, and the funeral was the same day of the meet and greet. We thought it through: If we left as soon as the service was over, we'd probably just make it in time to meet Jet, but we didn't want to race out of Paul's beloved aunt's funeral, so we decided to wait until December to meet Jet.

Eden was disappointed, but she understood—and maybe we could visit Jet another time as soon as we were approved. I just assumed we would be. I didn't expect to hear anything for a couple weeks and was pleasantly surprised to open our mailbox on the day before the funeral.

"Eden, it's a letter from the rescue!"

Eden ran downstairs, and I tore open the decidedly thick envelope—a surefire sign of good news if you're a college applicant but ambiguous for pug applicants.

I was confused. The envelope held our application. And there was a cover letter.

Dear Alison,

Enclosed, please find your incomplete application. Anyone we entrust with one of our fur children needs to be responsible and frankly, we consider your inability to completely answer all the questions a red flag.

If you want to fill out the rest of the information, we may reconsider your application.

Dwight Swanson

Don't Breed or Buy and Let Homeless Pugs Die!

I couldn't believe it. I looked through the pages of application I had carefully filled out. Dwight had highlighted my errors. I had forgotten to write down the telephone number for our veterinarian, as well as the twenty-four-hour emergency number and its name.

"He doesn't sound like a very nice man," Eden said.

"No," I responded, "he doesn't."

I was livid. He could take my incomplete application and shove it . . . I looked at Eden's worried face, and my anger dissipated.

"That's OK. I'll fill out everything I forgot, and we'll send it right back."

Which is exactly what I did, and then I wrote a gentler and kinder reply than the one I would have liked to have written.

Hi Dwight,

I hope you received Jack's record from our vet. [You know, the one with the glowing recommendation letter.] I've finished answering the [few, minute, hardly-worth-mentioning] things I previously forgot and will be getting this in the mail today. Eden, our eight-year-old and pug lover, fell and broke her arm this week [Aren't you ashamed of yourself for making such a mountain out of a molehill?], so it's been busy with extra doctor appointments. Also this week, my husband's aunt died [If you weren't ashamed before, you certainly should be now!], and the funeral is tomorrow here in Grand Rapids. We had planned to attend the meet and greet to see Jet, but I don't think we can possibly make it across the state in time. Are there any alternative times to meet him?

Thanks,

Alison

A couple weeks passed with no word, and then an email appeared in my inbox:

Subject: Adoption application

We have completed the review of your veterinary records, as well as the response to our letter. Your application has been approved. The next step is to tell us which of the pugs you would like to adopt. The only pug listed on the website that is no longer available because of a pending adoption is Bruno. Once you have made your choice, the pug you choose becomes a pending adoption contingent on your home visit. Let us know of your choice, and you will be contacted to schedule a home visit when you are both home.

Dwight Swanson

Don't Breed or Buy and Let Homeless Pugs Die!

I had already told him we were interested in Jet. Maybe he would have remembered that if he hadn't been running a background check that exceeded FBI standards. Would we need to be fingerprinted too? I did a little deep breathing and then wrote right back, summoning every bit of enthusiasm and self-control I could muster and quashing every ounce of snark, at least in the written form. My mind was still free and sassy.

This is great news!

We are interested in meeting Jet [as I've told you ten times already]. Would the home visit be someone bringing him here to meet us, or is it for you to "inspect" our house [which is beyond pug-friendly, thankyouverymuch]? I'm asking because if it is the latter, I would prefer to meet Jet first to guarantee that we want to proceed with the adoption. Unfortunately, we can't attend the meet and greet in December because my husband will be flying to Toronto that day. Is there a way we can see him another day? Also, I have some general questions that might be best answered by the foster home [you're not the only one with questions, Mister].

How do you recommend we proceed?

Thanks.

Alison

I received an almost immediate reply:

If you are interested in meeting Jet prior to making your decision, you will need to attend an event he will be at. The person doing your home visit will be from where you live. We do not do a home visit unless you have committed to adopting a particular pug.

What are your questions about Jet?

Now we were getting somewhere. I quickly wrote back all my questions.

We definitely want to meet him before we commit. I can check the website for his next meet and greet unless you know offhand. This is what I would like to know about Jet: What is his energy level? Does he enjoy walking? What is his temperament? Has he had any training? How often do his face creases need to be cleaned out? Is he prone to marking? He won't be alone very often, but there are rare occasions where we are away for a portion of the day. How long can he (comfortably) go without needing to be let outside? We have a black Lab, and we understand that it will be different with a smaller dog.

Thank you very much.

Alison

The responses were coming more quickly now.

Jet is walked each day. He is shy at first but warms up quickly. What kind of training are you referring to? If you are speaking of obedience, no. His face creases need to be cleaned out weekly. He is not prone to marking. We recommend crating. Most dogs do not mess in their crate. It is also advisable when there are multiple dogs that they be crated. Would you leave your children unsupervised?

I rolled my eyes. Of course I knew it was advisable that multiple dogs be crated. This last question really ticked me off. It was equal parts ridiculous and insulting. I immediately hit reply and began writing a testy response. Eden, as was her wont, was reading over my shoulder.

"Mama," she said, "would you please write another email that makes you sound less crazy?"

I did *not* want to write another email; if anything, I wanted to completely go off on this guy. I had eighteen months of rage ready to burn, and I had nothing to lose. If this guy withheld Jet, it didn't really matter: I still got the points for looking for a pug without (bonus!) actually having to adopt one. I looked at Eden. She was the one who had everything to lose, and if she did, I did too. I deleted my first email and started over.

Dwight,

Thank you very much.

Unfortunately, it appears we'll have to wait until the January meet and greet, since there isn't a way for us to drive across the state and make it home in time to make my husband's flight. This is frustrating since we were planning on November but couldn't make it because of our aunt's funeral. [Remember?!?]

We want to meet Jet before making a commitment. To do otherwise, we feel, would be irresponsible. For any dog we adopt, we will be committing for the long haul, which translates into—I hope!—at least a decade and likely thousands of dollars. We don't romanticize things. Our dog, Jack, has brought so much joy to our family and a lot of responsibility and expense too. We aren't adopting a second dog on a whim; we want to be thoughtful and responsible. Each dog is an individual. There are broad similarities within the breeds, but every dog is separate. I would think you would appreciate our understanding of this, our seriousness, and our commitment. [Anyone with a brain would too!]

I asked about Jet's needs specifically because I want to be as informed and prepared as possible. We know how to be responsible and loving owners of our black Lab, but what is appropriate for him won't be appropriate for a smaller dog and in particular for a pug. I know that we have to take extra care in the heat, so walking Jet in the summer will be brief and careful or nonexistent. Adapting to having a Lab and a pug, in that instance, isn't too difficult. This was why I asked about his exercise. We walk our Lab, but I'm guessing Jet won't be able to go as far and certainly not as fast. I'm thinking about how to meet his needs [because I am a loving and responsible dog owner!].

Regarding his bathroom needs—again—I want to understand how we would need to accommodate our schedule. We are rarely away. I am home all day, and when I'm gone, it's for an hour or two— and even then, someone is usually here. However, there are occasions when all of us are gone for extended periods of time, where it's not appropriate to take a dog, and I want to know how long we could leave Jet—comfortably—in a crate. We crated Jack the first couple of years, but now he is able to be free in the house safely, on all counts. Of course, we wouldn't leave our children unsupervised [you doofus], because we are responsible, which is why I want to know Jet's very specific needs.

So again, approximately how long can Jet go, comfortably, in his crate?

Thanks for your [nonexistent] consideration and patience as we try to be as prepared as possible.

Alison

The next day I received this reply.

Generally a pug can go 8 to 10 hours without an accident. Jet is in a foster home with a retired woman who is home most of the time. I don't think we can give you an accurate response to this question because of the circumstances with which he lives. Telling you anything other than what I have said would be grossly misrepresenting the situation.

We certainly wouldn't want him grossly misrepresenting the situation. I rolled my eyes for the hundredth time, and yet I was encouraged. A dog that could hold it for eight hours was a great sign. There was no way I was going to commit to adopt without meeting Jet, but I began to be genuinely encouraged that maybe a pug would truly work for our family.

A couple days later, Paul pulled me aside. "I called the airline, and I was able to switch to a later flight without paying a penalty. Do you want to go meet a little pug?"

We called the kids to the living room. Paul told them the good news by asking the same rhetorical question. They all shouted their agreement.

I emailed Dwight to find out if Jet was still available, and he responded later that night.

Yes we will be leaving promptly at 3:00 as I have a birthday party to be at for my grandson immediately after the meet and greet.
    Dwight Swanson

I immediately replied.

Great! We won't be able to get there until almost 2:00, but Jet will be there until 3:00, right?
    Thank you!
    Alison

I never heard back.

fifteen

The One That Got Away

Dear Pug List oh my goodness!
Thear is a new pug on petfinder.
he is Blak so my mom
and dad LOVE Him!
His name is Jet.
He is really really
Plump. and I Have
369.51! Yes I Do. and
I LOVE Him too. of corsh.

As soon as the buzzer rang at the end of Eden's basketball game the next morning, all five of us were out the door and jumping into the van. Eden didn't even want to take the time to change her clothes.

We arrived at the PetSmart a little after two o'clock. As soon as we entered the automatic doors, we saw a table with a sign: PUG RESCUE. A red-faced and visibly sweaty man stood beside it. Dwight.

I extended my hand and smiled. "Hi. I'm Alison. We're here to meet Jet."

Dwight shook his head. "You're ten minutes too late. You just missed him! A couple who have adopted with us in the past stopped by and said they wanted him." He smirked and pushed out his chest.

I stared. How was that possible? "But I told you we were on our way. My husband changed his flight . . ." I couldn't believe it. The dog had been available for weeks, months—but now just *minutes* before we got here . . . ?

"You knew we couldn't hold him. I'm sorry you had to drive all this way, but I tried to warn you."

He didn't sound a bit sorry. He sounded pleased. Well, bully for him. He hadn't won anything. I didn't really want the dog.

But I quailed when I turned to my children, who all looked heartbroken.

"Did they take him already?" I asked Dwight.

"Oh no. Jet's still here. You can meet him if you want."

"Do you want to?" I looked at the children. No one spoke. "We're here. We may as well meet him," I said. All three nodded and followed me over to the volunteers. When we said we had come to visit Jet, one went to get him from the other side of the store.

"He got a little overexcited, so Norma took him for a walk."

Just then he came tearing around the aisle, and we all crouched down to greet him. He bounded up, snorting and breathing so heavily it sounded like he was about to have a stroke. Eden bent to hug him, and he barreled into her. She was on her knees, and she crouched over him, encircling him with her arms, burying her head next to his. He stood calmly. Tongue stuck out, panting. I could feel my resolve against a second dog weakening. I pulled out my camera and took a picture just before he broke free from Eden and ran into Lydia, who caught him in her arms. She looked to the volunteers.

"May I hold him?" she asked with her usual good manners.

"Oh, sure. Of course!" they said at once.

Lydia carefully picked him up and held his face next to hers. After Lydia set him down, she and Eden sat on the floor, and he scurried between them. Christopher held back a bit, watching. It was impossible not to smile.

"What a hoot!" I said to the woman standing closest to me.

"Your children are so good with him," she said.

"They've always been dog lovers," I said and then explained about Jack and how hard we had all worked to train him.

She introduced herself. Her name was Norma. She had been fostering Jet. "He's the sweetest little dog. And to be honest, I have gotten very attached to him. I heard a family was coming to see him today, and that was the only thing that made it bearable—thinking about him being with a nice family."

We looked over at the children all huddled around Jet, petting him but being careful not to crowd him. His tail was wagging, and he looked cheerful. He was clearly happy and comfortable.

Eden looked up. "Is it OK if we walk him around the store?" Norma said it was fine, and Jet trotted off with the girls.

I looked back at Norma. "I asked Dwight if there was any way we could meet Jet outside of a meet and greet, and he said it wasn't possible. We didn't want to disturb you or be a hassle, but we really wanted to meet him before we committed."

Norma pressed a palm to her chest. "I wouldn't have minded having you come over. I wouldn't have minded at all. He is just the sweetest little dog. I've never let a dog up on my bed, but he barely shed, so I slept with him every night. I'm going to miss him so much."

Hold up. I leaned in. "He barely sheds? I thought pugs were nonstop shedders."

"The fawn ones are—with their double coats—but the black ones have single coats and shed so much less. With Jet, there were just a few hairs here and there."

My mouth suddenly became dry. I swallowed before asking, "Is he housebroken?"

Norma nodded. "He sure is. He never had an accident. He would go right to the door and give a bark, and I'd get him outside, and we never had a problem."

I felt sick.

She leaned in and dropped her voice. "That couple barely even spent any time with Jet. They just walked in, looked at him for a minute, said they would take him, and left. You all have spent more time with him than they did." She leaned in even closer. "One of the other volunteers and I asked Dwight to wait for you. He told us you were coming, and we couldn't understand why he wouldn't just wait."

"I don't think Dwight is a fan," I said, and then I told her about all the emails and my hesitation to commit before I met Jet. I told her about the funeral and the changed flight. I told her about the fire and Eden working for more than a year to earn the money. Just then, Eden and Lydia came bounding back with Jet.

"Mama, do you want to hold him?" Eden asked.

"Sure!" I smiled at Norma and knelt down next to Lydia, who scooped up Jet and carefully lowered him into my arms. Jet looked this way and that, snorting and breathing heavily. I hugged him to me. His heart was pounding a million beats a minute. I felt a surge of affection for this adorable, friendly, low-shedding, completely housebroken gem of a dog.

I handed the camera to Lydia and passed Jet to Eden, who hugged him tightly while I put my arms around her. In the picture I'm laughing. Eden is half-hidden because Jet's face is right in front, and he's looking eager and alert, ears cocked, ready for anything.

I saw Norma and Shirley huddled a few feet away in a whispered conference, and then Norma returned.

"Shirley is just as upset as I am. She called Dwight's wife to let her know what happened, and she's coming over."

Paul was talking to Dwight, while Christopher stood off to the side.

"Don't you want to meet Jet?" I asked Christopher.

He shook his head. "Once I realized Jet was already adopted, I decided I didn't want to get too close to him because it hurts too much." Tears filled his eyes.

"Oh, buddy." I gave him a hug and patted his back. "Why don't you go over? I think you'll regret it if you don't." Christopher nodded and headed over to his sisters.

Paul excused himself, and it was just Dwight and me.

"The kids sure do love dogs," Dwight said.

"Yup." I said. I'm not great with small talk anyway—and certainly not with people I want to smack.

"It's really important that the whole family knows how to treat animals. We had this one situation with a family with three little kids, and one of the children was deathly afraid of dogs."

He launched into a meandering story about a pug he placed in a home a monkey could have predicted wasn't going to work out, and then—*oh, wait a minute!*—the family had to surrender the pug, and this was terrible for the dog, who had already been rehomed once before—"and we just really try to avoid situations where it's not going to be a good fit."

I stared. This was the man who had been pressuring me for a month to commit to a dog I'd never met.

"I completely understand. That's why I wanted to meet Jet," I said slowly. "I wanted to make sure he would be a good fit for our family. Once we commit to a pug, we don't plan to surrender him."

This was when Dwight finally got it. It was almost as if a lightbulb went on over his head. I was no longer that woman bugging him with her incessant emails. I suddenly became a good and loving home for one of his beloved "fur children."

"You know, I feel really bad about you coming all this way. I have another pug you should meet. Howie's foster family lives right around the corner. What if I called them and asked if they could bring him over?"

I had seen Howie. He was fawn, and besides, all I wanted to do was grab Jet and make a break for the van. But I figured we might as well meet any pug we could.

I shrugged. "OK," I said.

An older woman came in, and Norma and Shirley made a beeline for her. I saw them huddle together, and then she approached Dwight. It must have been the wife.

Howie arrived soon after, and we all met him and petted him. He was a sweet dog, but he wasn't Jet. We all felt it.

And then it was three o'clock and time to go. We all said good-bye to Jet, who was just as excited as he had been when we arrived.

I thanked Norma for being so kind.

"He's not budging," she whispered.

"I'm going to email him and plead," I whispered back.

"Let me know about Howie," Dwight called after us and waved.

The mood in the van home fluctuated between anger and sorrow. After a little while, Eden announced, "We should be thankful for what we do have."

"What's that?" I asked, not really sure what she meant.

"Jackie Boy!"

We all agreed we had a lot to be thankful for in already having one good dog. I was impressed.

"Well, I'm thankful to have a girl with such a great attitude."

We dropped off Paul at the airport just in time. The kids and I spent a quiet evening at home. We were all feeling down. Eden asked if she could email her dad. She carefully typed.

> Dear daddy, I reeeeeeeeeeeeeeally miss you. did you get the fancy hotel soap?:) well ok please listen, did you love jet? or did you just love us, and not want to hurt our feelings. I don't want us to have a dog that you have no part of. that you do not like. daddy I wrote this my self. love Eden. Bye-bye.

I loved this. It was just a little email, and yet so much more. I loved her concern about Paul; the wisdom in knowing that parents often go along with things for the pleasure it brings our children, for love.

" . . . that you have no part of. that you do not like." It's so easy to just want something and not really care about another person's needs and wishes.

And then, "daddy I wrote this my self." This undid me.

Paul replied almost immediately.

> Aw, thank you for your note, Eden. I miss you a lot too. I've got some soap and it's a little fancy—you can be the judge. I thought Jet was adorable, and I'm sure I would love him a lot too if he was ours. You're so sweet to ask me. I love you. Bye-bye, angel.

After the kids were in bed, I reopened my laptop and got to work. It was time to play the fire card. And I was about to smack it down hard.

> Dear Dwight,
>
> I'd like to share something with you.
>
> We had a house fire a year ago. We lost everything and had to tear down our old house. Here is the newspaper coverage.

I included the link to the pictures of our house in flames.

I went on to tell him about the fire, how traumatic it had been, and what a long, hard road we had all traveled on our way back to a different normal. I told him about Eden and her Pug Fund, about how hard she had worked, and, most importantly, about how she had never given up hope.

Yesterday, going to see Jet was a sign that things were normal again, that we were finally starting over. I can't tell you how much it hurt my kids to meet Jet, knowing that he had been given to someone else only minutes before we arrived.

I reminded him that we had wanted to come in November and that it was only because of a funeral that we couldn't be there. I reminded him of all we had rescheduled to make it that day.

My husband and I can deal with the hassle, the gas and the wasted time, but it's the pain to our children that's so hard. Our son, Christopher, purposely didn't spend a lot of time with Jet because he was so sad to hear he had been adopted out.

I wonder if you got impatient with me for not wanting to commit to a picture and for asking questions. I was trying to do my due diligence. You did yours, figuring out if we would be a good home for one of your pugs, and I needed to do mine to make sure that Jet would be a good fit with us and our dog. My husband and I are responsible. We aren't going to surrender a beloved pet. We will work with, invest in, and love any pug we adopt or buy.

Would you please reconsider your decision?

Thank you.

Alison Hodgson

Allison [of course he misspelled my name],

I am sorry you feel that this was a punishment to you and your family, and I am truly sorry to hear of the tragedies of your recent past. We did nothing different in the case of Jet than we do with any other pug that is in our organization. The first family that indicated they want to adopt the pug that has an approved application is the one that gets the pug.

He told me about all the people who had come by and expressed interest in Jet, including one woman who ran to her vet's office to pick up records. Since there were no other events until January, he offered to set up a personal meeting with any other pug we might be interested in. *Now he was willing!*

152 The Pug List

I did feel bad about the situation, but I also cannot tell someone else who has an approved application that they cannot adopt a particular pug on the basis that someone else is coming to see the pug and may wish to adopt it.

Our process is a first-come, first-served basis (for approved applicants). [Well, I guess that works for McDonald's. But these are animals, not hamburgers, Dwight!] If you were to arrive and indicate you did not want that pug, or for some reason never arrived, then the opportunity to get a "forever home" for that pug may be lost because the other family goes elsewhere.

He apologized for my feeling that his process was unfair, and then he went on to defend it for another paragraph—blah, blah, blah—before he got to the bottom line,

... but I cannot now tell the other family that they cannot have Jet.
Dwight Swanson
Don't Breed or Buy and Let Homeless Pugs Die!

So that was that. Looking back, I can see his point. *I* knew we were on the way. I was clear on the seriousness of our commitment, with the pint-sized pug lover willing us forward. But Dwight didn't, and people can be flakes. Every single day, people don't do what they say they're going to do. If anyone knew that, it was the director of a dog rescue. I'm willing to give Dwight the benefit of the doubt now. But I wasn't then.

sixteen

Another Orphan Named Oliver

We took a week to lick our wounds. We looked at the dozens of pictures I took of Jet. I walked around the house calling Jet's name like Rocky Balboa calling for Adrian. I thought over what I could have done differently. I should have said yes. Why did I change my mind? *Why* didn't I say yes? I should have said yes. Ugh.

I emailed the director of the local rescue where I had found Tonka. I told her about the fire and about Eden. I told her about Jet and the other rescue and asked if she ever got black pugs.

She wrote back right away. She remembered me and told me she would keep an eye out for black pugs.

I got online and began to search for breeders. The few I found in Michigan were either between litters or only had fawn puppies available. I expanded my search, and a farm came up in Ohio, less than an hour from Toledo. Puppies were available, but I didn't even check them out because right there on the home page, in a sidebar, was a picture of an adult black pug with a stern little face, staring straight into the camera. "Outrageous Oliver," the caption read.

I could feel my heartbeat. We were already planning a trip to Toledo to visit friends for New Year's. I immediately thought of discovering Jack in Kalamazoo two days before we planned to spend the day there. This had the same "by the pricking of my thumbs" feeling of synchronicity or serendipity, maybe even providence. I called Eden to take a look. There was no point in taking another step without her approval.

She said he was cute and worth checking out. Later she confessed she took one look and thought, *I know we're going to take home this dog.*

"Yes," she said, "let's go visit."

I carefully composed an email to the breeder, taking extra care to sound normal and yet ask the vital questions.

My name is Alison Hodgson. My family is interested in purchasing a black pug. Would you tell me a little bit about Oliver? We have a four-year-old English black Lab, who is what we call a "dog's dog," whose best friend at the home where we board him is a fawn pug. [Subtext: We have dog experience and—bonus—our dog has pug experience!] My husband and I have three children, 16, 14, and 9, all of whom are comfortable with and respectful of dogs, but our household is loud and energetic. [It's mayhem by any other name, but I don't want to scare you.] Is Oliver at all anxious or nervous? Does he have any problems with marking? [For the love of God, is he housebroken? I just can't deal with a dog that isn't housebroken.] We live in Michigan but will be in Toledo for New Year's weekend. Would it work for us to come to the farm Friday the 30th or Sunday January 1? We would love to meet and get to know Oliver. [I really need to nail down the whole potty issue in person.]

I heard nothing. We were busy with Christmas, our first one in the new house, and I didn't think too much about Oliver. I did wonder if someone had bought him and the owner was too busy or just didn't want the bother of writing back to let me know. In a way, I was relieved. As the time from meeting Jet passed, my passion abated. Once again, I was thankful to get all the credit for pursuing a pug without actually having one. We could wait.

A couple days before we left for Toledo, an email arrived in my inbox.

Hello Alison,

Sorry it took so long to get back to you. I would love to tell you more about Oliver if you would like to call me.

Melissa

I called that night.

"I've only had him for a year," Melissa said. "I drove down south to buy a silver pug from a breeder in another state. He had Oliver in a tiny outdoor kennel. The conditions were terrible. His whole life was spent in that cage outside. I didn't need another male, but there was just something about Oliver. The breeder said if I bought the silver, he'd throw in Oliver free, and I couldn't leave him there. I wish I could keep him. I love him, but he doesn't get along with my alpha male. I thought I had a place for him a few months ago. It was a woman, and she was nice, but she called me the first night because Oliver was huddled under the table. She had another dog, and Oliver seemed afraid of him. I told her that Oliver probably just needed a little time to adjust, but she was so stressed-out that I asked her if she wanted to bring him back, and she did."

I told Melissa our story about the fire, about how hard it had been, about Eden longing for a pug and working for a year to earn the money.

"Alison, the only reason I said he was for sale was to weed out bad people. I just want to find him a good home. If it's a good fit, I would be happy to give him to you."

I had known Eden would someday learn you can work and work and work and still not get what you want, and so too, there are times you are given more than you could hope for or imagine. She had had so much taken away from her—her childhood home, her favorite things, her sense of security. But the one thing she wanted the most—and had worked so hard to earn—was now being given to her as a gift. Would this pug—this "Outrageous Oliver"—be what she needed to heal her heart and spirit? Tears streamed down my face.

And yet, even in the face of almost certain providence, I still had my gleaming wood floors and new carpets to consider.

"Is he housebroken?"

"He wasn't for the first three years. He was never let out of that cage, but he's a smart little dog. When he came to my house, I trained him. He had a few accidents in the beginning, but he's crate-trained and has been doing just fine for a year."

I exhaled. We could work with this. Melissa and I decided to meet on Sunday morning, January 1.

A couple days later, we pulled up in front of a small house in an older neighborhood. As we gathered on Melissa's porch, I had that nervous, first-date feeling. Melissa opened the door and invited us to sit down in the living room. Paul, Christopher, Lydia, and I all squeezed together on the sofa. Eden sat on the floor at our feet.

There were several pugs in the room, and I tried to identify Oliver. Some of them were elderly and not very cute. Looks aren't everything, of course, and goodness knows, a pug is not a traditional beauty, but I hoped to have that click with the one we adopted. A little black one trotted in.

Melissa pointed. "This is Oliver." He looked around, eager and interested. He was skinny but definitely cute. He was darling, actually. The girls and I immediately began gushing. He came right up to Eden. As if he knew! My heart was in my throat. My little girl's years of prayers and hard, hard work were finally being answered and rewarded. And then he lifted his back leg and peed on her coat.

This is what they call a red flag.

"Oliver!" Melissa shouted.

I hopped off the sofa. I felt awkward because he wasn't our dog, but if he was going to be, I knew I needed to take charge. I grabbed him and gently flipped him on his back. One of my dog books recommended this as a way to easily establish who's in charge. He squirmed and fought, but I held on. He stared right at me, unrepentant. What an intense and absurd little face! I was accustomed to Jack's handsome and benign countenance. This creature could be an alien.

"Uh-oh!" I said calmly but firmly and motioned Eden to come over.

"Uh-oh!" she said just the same.

Oliver stared back and then looked away. Eventually something in him loosened, and he relaxed. I let go, and he jumped up. Meanwhile, Melissa had brought in a bottle of Nature's Miracle, an enzyme spray for cleaning up pet accidents and eliminating any odors. She sprayed Eden's coat and wiped up the floor.

"This stuff is amazing. You'll want to get some of it right away." Red flag! Red flag!

Oliver sat on Eden's lap and let her pet him. He was docile and definitely adorable.

And then he lifted his leg and peed. Again.

"Oliver!" Melissa shouted, and we ran the drill: She sprayed and dabbed. I rolled and held the dog. Eden said "Uh-oh!" Oliver stared back, mulish and obdurate. Eventually, again, he relaxed, and I released him.

We decided that Oliver recognized Eden as the smallest and possibly weakest of our family and was just trying to establish his place.

"He *is* stubborn," Melissa said. "He may test you." Red flag! Red flag! Red flag!

We nodded as if hypnotized. Yes, that made perfect sense. We understood. Why this did not register as a problem I can't say—even when Melissa assembled the few things she had kindly provided: a new harness and leash, a couple days' supply of food, and a little blue cloth wrap she called a bellyband.

"What's that?" I asked.

"Oh, it's to prevent marking, just to be on the safe side on the ride home and maybe the first few days in the house."

Now, I'm a reader, a voracious one, and ever since I was a child, foreshadow has leapt off the page. For as long as I can remember, I have known when an author tells you something, it's for a reason. Do I need to explain that Melissa's sending Oliver off—a dog that has allegedly been house-trained for a year—wearing a quasi-dog-diaper is a red flag so large that a toreador could have used it to summon a bull?

Anyone with an ounce of sense would recognize this as an ominous sign.

But we didn't. It's as if a force beyond reason was compelling us. With Jack's adoption, we went out to lunch to privately and carefully decide. Even after meeting his plump, adorable self, we soberly discussed whether or not he was the right dog for us. This time, there was no discussion. Without a word, we all knew we were going to take this funny little dog home.

"Just for a trial," I said, my nails scraping the edge of the cliff.

"You can always bring him back," Melissa said reassuringly.

Eden carried Oliver to the van. She and Lydia climbed into the backseat and bundled him into her comforter. His breathing was fast and heavy. We had read about how loudly pugs breathe, but it sounded as if Oliver was in the final stretch of a triathlon. We were all nervous he would have a stroke. Lydia and Eden petted him gently. Eventually he relaxed, and his breathing calmed.

I looked back, and Oliver's little face was peeking out of Eden's comforter, his tongue stuck out and lolling to the side. Eden's head was down and resting on his head. Her falling hair obscured half of her face, but from what I could see, her expression was one of longing fulfilled.

seventeen

Tween Mother

By the time we got home from Toledo, Oliver knew who his girl was, and he wasn't going to let her out of his sight. From the moment they walked out of the van, he was by her side. They were inseparable. Wherever Eden went, he followed closely in her wake. The sound of his little nails clicking soon became the accompaniment to Eden's every movement. Better yet, she carried him around, and he didn't protest, even slightly.

"Wherever thou goest" seemed to be Oliver's heart's cry, and he was up for anything Eden had in mind. The first morning home, I walked downstairs and saw her sitting at our island, eating a bowl of cereal. Oliver was perched on a stool next to her, perfectly content to keep an eye on her. Later that afternoon, I found them on her bed. Eden had plunked Oliver in her lap and was singing a song she learned for school. She waved his little paws back and forth to do the motions, and Oliver leaned against her like a limp puppet, perfectly tolerable to everything. His only controlled movement was blinking.

"Do you think it's love or Stockholm syndrome?" I asked Paul.

"Who can say? Perhaps something in between."

Right from the start, Eden let us know she was Oliver's mother. "*You* are his grandparents."

Paul and I tried to dissuade her. We just didn't see ourselves as the sort of people who were dog "parents," let alone grandparents. That just wasn't our style. Sure, we gave Jack his own "voice" with which he'd call us "Mommy" and "Daddy" in a plaintive tone. But that was a joke! Mere silliness!

Eden persisted. *She* was the only reason we had Oliver, and please don't forget, *she* had worked for more than a year to rescue him.

Regardless of how you defined their relationship, they both knew they belonged together. Oliver was Eden's dog, and she took her responsibility seriously. The first business day after our return, she personally called the vet to schedule an appointment. Oliver cuddled up next to her on the sofa while she talked. The receptionist, who had been following our pug journey, was delighted to hear we had adopted him.

"We're on a trial," I said in the background, but Eden ignored me—and who was I kidding?

Since Melissa so graciously gave Oliver to us, Paul and I discussed what Eden should do with her Pug Fund. I assumed we would let her keep it, but Paul disagreed.

"I think she should use it to help with some of his expenses. Having an animal is more than just playing with it and having fun; it's also the costs and responsibilities. It's a combination. She's going to care for him and feed and groom him too. If she wants to own this dog, she's going to share the responsibility. It's an important part of growing up."

This made sense to me, and when we talked to Eden about it, she readily agreed.

At Oliver's first appointment, she took the lead. All the questions were directed to her, and she answered everything in her calm and intelligent way. We adults exchanged smiles over her head. She sat upright with Oliver on her lap, a look of utter seriousness on her sweet face.

We were accustomed to Jack, who literally ran to the vet's—anything to be with other dogs. We assumed Oliver's veterinary experience was limited, but nothing could have prepared us for what exactly that meant.

The technician lifted Oliver onto the metal table, separating him from his girl. Strike one. He began to whimper. Eden looked at me, her lips pursed in a frown. It's hard to see your little one in discomfort and duress. The vet and the technician were efficient. Calmly and quickly, the vet examined him while the technician held Oliver tight.

But then it was time to trim his nails, and that's when Oliver went ballistic. Eyes wild, his legs shot in four directions. He was clawing and trying to tear his way free. Tongue out, panting. And the sound he made was otherworldly, something between a yowl and a roar.

"It's OK, Oliver. I'm right here," Eden assured him.

"Do you want me to help hold him down?" I asked. What this little pug lacked in size he made up for in stubborn strength.

"I've got him," the technician said. She adjusted her hold; the vet quickly finished up and released him.

Eden rushed to his side. Oliver was gasping.

"Good boy, Oliver!"

"What a brave boy!"

"All done now! You're OK!"

"That's a good boy!"

We all showered praise, and the doctor gave him a treat. Eden cuddled him while the doctor and I discussed next steps. When I asked how soon he could be neutered, she recommended he have an alar fold resection at the same time.

"What's that?"

"Basically I make two small slits in his nostrils to help him breathe. It's a common procedure for pugs and other brachycephalic breeds."

The pug needed a nose job. Of course. This just seemed to be our way with dogs. Jack was our last-of-the-litter steal, who turned out to be no bargain. And now Oliver was our free dog, but I guess there really is no such thing as a free lunch—or pug. We made an appointment for both procedures for later in the month. When I saw the estimate for them, along with all the shots he would need to get up-to-date, I was glad we had Eden's Pug Fund to soften the blow.

A couple days later, just as Oliver and Eden were going to bed, he gagged and threw up. Eden shouted for me. I grabbed Oliver, ran downstairs, and shoved him outside. He stood on the back porch and stared at me through the French doors. It was so cold that after about a minute, I took pity and opened the door.

I brought him back upstairs. I prayed with Eden and tucked her in. Oliver had immediately fallen asleep at her feet. He seemed fine. I walked back to my bedroom. Within minutes, Eden was calling for me. We met in the hall, where Oliver threw up at our feet.

"Poor baby!" This was Eden talking. *I* was thinking about my poor floors and went to get paper towel and Nature's Miracle. Eden dutifully cleaned up the mess while I looked up Oliver's symptoms on petmd. com. The gagging reminded me a lot of Jack's bruised trachea, although he never actually expelled anything; he just coughed and coughed and coughed. And Ollie didn't throw down his chow the way Jack did.

With Oliver's smooshed little face, eating was quite an endeavor. He liked his food but had to work for every bite. First he picked up several pieces of kibble and dropped them on the floor; then carefully, one at a time, he chomped with his head tilted, seemingly with only half his jaw, chewing and chewing each one to bits. A bruised trachea wasn't likely, and there was the fact that Oliver actually threw up every few minutes.

"Let's stay here," I suggested. I pulled off a few paper towels and set them in front of Oliver to catch anything. After each effluence, I swiped the messed towels and made a new little mat.

By now, Paul and Christopher and Lydia joined us. Christopher and Lydia gently petted Oliver. We sat in a circle with Oliver next to Eden, who slumped against Paul or me.

After an hour or so, Christopher and Lydia excused themselves. "Maybe you should just get to bed," I told Eden. "Daddy and I can stay up with him." She slipped into her room when Oliver wasn't looking, but there was no fooling him. He scratched at the door and whined.

Eden got out of bed and sat back down with a sigh. We could debate what she was to him, but it was clear: He needed her always. This was the price of complete devotion. Eventually the time between heave sessions lengthened and finally stopped. Paul and I tucked the two of them into bed and fell into our own.

The next morning, Oliver was at it again, and I called the vet first thing. As I was describing the symptoms, Oliver gagged and retched.

"Stop right there," the receptionist said. "I don't even need to talk to the doctor. That's kennel cough. We'll get you a prescription, and you can pick it up in just a little bit."

He had just been vaccinated for kennel cough—and then immediately developed it. So it goes.

He had some accidents here and there, but we chalked it up to the stress of the adjustment. Any time one was discovered, Eden ran to get the paper towel and spray. She cheerfully dispatched mess after mess.

After Oliver's surgeries, she lovingly and patiently cared for him.

When we picked him up from the vet, he was wearing a little cone that was even smaller than the one Jack had for this same surgery when he was a puppy. Oliver's little black face peeked out of it, and at four years, he looked more like a puppy than Jack had at four months.

Since Oliver still wasn't entirely reliable in the potty department, we had him sleeping in a little kennel we placed next to Eden's bed. During the day, we could (mostly) keep an eye on him, but at night all bets were off. He didn't like it, but being so close to Eden seemed to make up for being imprisoned. The night of the procedures, Eden tucked Oliver in like normal, but he was not going for it. She managed to get him into the kennel, but once she shut the door, he began to whimper.

I was accustomed to this pathetic sound, but this was the first time Eden had heard it.

"Mama, he's so sad!"

"I know. That's just how he sounds when he's upset. Just give him a minute. He'll settle down."

He didn't.

"Mama, he won't stop!"

I peered into the kennel, and the saddest little face, framed by that ridiculous cone, stared back. He sneezed. I didn't think he could look more pathetic, but he did.

"May we please let him out just for tonight?"

"OK, just for tonight."

Famous last words.

"Just for tonight" became one more and then another and then just until the cone came off—and by then, we all knew that Oliver was Eden's permanent bedmate.

What I didn't notice until much later was that Eden's regular and frequent crying sessions were becoming less and less common. Since Oliver, there hadn't been one.

In fact, Eden was cheerful most days. She used my computer for school, and one day, I saw two new videos in my Photo Booth. One showed her singing "Lollipop! Lollipop!" at the top of her lungs, with a huge smile on her face. I didn't know it was possible to smile with your entire face while you were singing, but she did it. The other showed her in front of a backdrop that made it look like she was in Paris, with the Eiffel Tower in the background. I hit Play.

"As you can see, I'm in France. It's a beauuuuutiful place." She giggled, seemingly drunkenly. "And my little puppy Oliver's right here. Let me go grab him." She slid sideways and out of view and then returned, hoisting Oliver. "I brought him to France with me." His cone blocked most of his face, and his front paws were stuck out in front. "He's wearing his invisible cone," she said in a cooing voice, wobbling back and forth. "You can't really see him; he's sleepwalking," she said as she stumbled backward, trying to heave him up. Oliver snored audibly. "Sorry about that," she whispered. "He's sleepwalking. Good—" The video stopped abruptly.

There were dozens of still photos. Oliver and Eden at the kitchen island. Oliver and Eden on her bed. Oliver and Eden on the sofa. Oliver and Eden on my bed. In every one, her smile lit up the frame.

I hadn't realized how much I had missed that smile until I saw it again.

We got Oliver on January 1. Eden's birthday is January 25. Within days of bringing him home, she was composing her wish list.

> Dog clothes for Oliver
> Money to buy clothes for Oliver
> Gift certificates to Chow Hound

There seemed to be a theme.

"Do you have any other suggestions?" I asked.

"Nope." Her complete clarity gave me pause. Planning to spend her birthday money on clothes for her baby? As someone who's no stranger to placing my children's wants and needs before my own, I was convinced.

"She's his mother," I told Paul, and he finally agreed.

We still balked at being his grandparents, and I truly believe we would have held fast, except for one tiny, little thing: We talked on behalf of our dogs incessantly.

It started long before Jack and Oliver, however. As soon as Christopher was born, I had fun saying silly and impertinent things in Baby Christopher voice to make Paul laugh. Because of his deafness,

Christopher was late to speech, which gave us more time to speak for him. Soon Lydia was born, and we could each take a part, but not for long. Lydia, who had the benefit of normal hearing, as well as an oral-deaf education, learned to speak quickly and precociously, and by then, even Christopher's speech developed and expanded.

When Eden was born, Paul and I were back at it with a vengeance. But like her sister, all too soon she was speaking for herself, and she had a lot to say. When we got Jack, we were happy to know we finally had someone with whom we could go the long haul—and it was pure delight to make up things for him to say. Jack, while a golden boy of a dog, was clearly no intellectual, and it was fun to speak in the silly and simple voice we imagined was his.

When Oliver joined the family, we welcomed having another character to give voice to. To Oliver, Eden became "Mommy"; Paul became "Grandpappy"; and I—well, I hesitate to even tell you what Oliver came to call me.

The children had grown up hearing us speak for their siblings or Jack, and they were quick to jump in with Oliver. Eden knew—you talk for your children and your dog. In her case, it was one and the same, and she was on top of it. Nonstop. How she spoke for him—her "Oliver accent," if you will—varied. She started with a regular baby voice. With her being a rookie and Oliver such a small dog, anyone could understand that choice. Soon she got creative and began to affect a British accent for him, the poshness of which was so fluid that it varied from word to word.

"Bobby!" I heard "Oliver" say with a decidedly British accent, "would you wike to have tea and twumpets wif me?"

"I would *love* to have tea and crumpets with you, Oliver," Eden said. "He can't pronounce his 'l's' or his 'm's,'" she whispered as an aside.

"Bobby is supposed to be Mommy?"

"Yesh!" she/he replied.

"That's ridiculous. 'Mama' is one of the first things most babies say." Because I was for upholding the most logical and realistic talking on behalf of dogs. Standards, you know!

"It's *nawt* ridickweeous."

But before I knew it, I was answering to *three* names within our household: Alison, Mama, and Grandbobby.

I was glad Eden was homeschooled that year, because Oliver hated to be without her. In the first few weeks after we got him, he was inconsolable whenever Eden left him. While she was gone, he went from window to window, climbing up on his back paws to look for her, whining with those wild, anxious eyes all the while. After about a month, he adjusted. He didn't like it, but he reached a level of acceptance. To cope, he would find me and snuggle in—or if I was on the go, he'd follow me everywhere. If I was gone, he moved on to Lydia.

I grew accustomed to his attachment routine until one day, with both dogs along, I dropped Eden off for an appointment with her math tutor. As Eden climbed out of the van, Oliver scurried to the front seat and put his front paws on the window. I expected whining, but the sound he made was so strange that I put the van in park and called Paul at work.

"What is that sound?" he asked

A coworker heard him and got up from her desk, intrigued and concerned.

"It's Oliver. We just dropped Eden off at Mathnasium, and Puggy is not pleased."

"It sounds like a goat being strangled."

"I know. I've never heard anything like it."

Clearly, it was one thing for Oliver to be left at home, but it was another entirely to abandon his girl. Not on *his* watch.

But whenever Eden returned, oh—it became a three-ring circus.

Oliver would bolt to the door, running in circles, bouncing on all four paws like a pogo-stick pug, and finally throwing his head back and howling, "A-whoo! Whoo! Whoo!" Circle again. "Whoo! Whoo! Whoo!" Who could resist that sort of welcome?

And yet, like so many mothers before her, sometimes Eden craved a break. One night, just before bed, she was lounging in my bedroom, with Oliver right beside her, snoring loudly. Eden quietly got up and crept out of the room. She barely made it to the door before Oliver, feeling her absence, hopped off the bed and scampered after her.

She brought him back and tucked him under a throw. After a few minutes, she crept off again, and within seconds, he was following her down the hall.

"Oliver!" She picked him up and yet again set him on our bed. I noticed what was going on.

"Were you trying to ditch him?"

"Yes!"

"Why?" This was weird. They slept together every night.

"I'm exhausted, Mama! I haven't had a good night's sleep since we got him."

"You haven't?" From the time she was a newborn, Eden had been an excellent sleeper.

"He hogs the bed. I can't stretch my legs. And no matter where I try to move him to, he scoots right next to me!" She was on the verge of tears. I thought of those dolls that are given to high school students to simulate teen parenting and wondered if the simulation would be more effective if they were issued pugs instead. This tween mother could be a spokesperson.

"I'll keep him here, and you go get into bed. Shut my door and yours."

"Thank you, Mama."

I scratched Oliver's belly, and he stretched on his back for a moment or two until he perceived the change in the force, rolled over, and hopped off the bed. He stood in front of the closed door and scratched.

I looked up from my book. "No, Oliver."

The scratching paused, but only for a moment.

"Oliver! No!" I got out of bed and picked him up. I tried to hold him, but he wiggled out of my grasp.

"Oliver." I opened the door to see what he would do. He made a mad dash down the hall and stood in front of Eden's door. He sat at attention and simply stared, as if willing the door to open. He looked so tiny and pathetic. I went to pick him up and take him back to my room, but then I heard Eden.

"Just forget it. He can come in."

I opened her door, and Oliver shot across her room and jumped onto her bed, quickly settling in beside her, his little head resting on his paws, dark eyes shining before they relaxed and slowly blinked shut. Eden rolled over, tossing an arm above her head, and letting out a big sigh. Tween mothering a pug was clearly an overwhelming task at times, but I knew the benefits far outweighed the challenges.

I have wondered why Oliver bonded immediately and irrevocably with Eden. A cynical person may be tempted to dismiss their bond with the argument that dogs are pack animals and pugs are companion dogs; they crave the presence of their people especially. While this was true, it didn't explain why he chose Eden, but I'm so glad he did.

One day I saw a paper on our table with Eden's distinctive handwriting.

Dress up Oliver 2:30
go outside 2:50
Dance to Adele 4:00
tatoos 4:40
Hi Dad! 5:00
eat dinner 5:10 (yuck!)
Do nails 6:00
Climb a tree 6:50

It was clearly a schedule for her after-school activities, and despite her commentary on my cooking, I smiled, so happy to read it.

When Oliver first came, if Paul and I had sat down with him to list our hopes for his relationship with Eden and establish some best pug practices, or just to share our prayers and dreams, they might have looked something like this:

Love our girl.

Allow her to love you.

Help heal her heart.

That night, as I shut her bedroom door, I knew, without a doubt, we could have checked off every item on the list.

eighteen

A Tinier Case of Post-Traumatic Stress

I regret to say there's a but.

Or rather there's a butt—a little black furry one.

I don't like the word *poop*. Whether verb or noun, I don't like to think of it. And yet, there it was, all too often, in a corner of our basement or in neat little piles on the rug by the back door. "Eden!" whoever spotted it yelled, and she dutifully came running with paper towels and the trusty Nature's Miracle.

What was so shocking was the volume. Despite the fact that Oliver was a quarter of Jack's size, his excrement was not proportionally smaller. How could such a small dog produce so much waste?

"Oh yeah," a friend who has several French bulldogs commiserated. "Frenchies and pugs are notorious for their enormous poops." What a terrible notoriety. In all the books and websites I'd read, there had never been a warning.

Stinky piles of poo were bad enough; it was the pee that was intolerable. Oh, the humanity. Oliver decided early on that Christopher's room was a good place to nip into and go potty. "It *is* a very stinky place!" Eden said in her baby's defense. Boots in the mudroom were another favorite spot. Eden's snow pants were a common target—and every so often, a piece of furniture. This was a problem.

In fact, this was a thousand times worse than my nightmare of even more black hair spread on every floor.

"He lived in an outdoor kennel for three years!" His mother was his staunch defender. "He doesn't understand."

Looking into Oliver's big and unblinking eyes, I thought he understood just fine. We kept a fairly close eye on him when we were home, but the few occasions on which the entire family was away were problematic.

He had his kennel, but he hated it. When we left the house, Eden had to push him into it and shut the door quickly. We were never gone for more than a couple hours, but it was terrible to leave him whining and crying loudly. The first time we returned, we could hear his labored breathing as soon as we walked in the back door. The crate was halfway across the living room. Eden ran to open it. There was a puddle in the bottom.

"Oliver!" we both cried out. *He even wet his own kennel!*

I ran to get the paper towel while Eden cuddled the pathetic thing. I mopped up the mess.

I looked at it with a sudden realization. "This isn't pee," I said.

Oliver was still breathing heavily. "I think it's saliva," Eden said. She was right. He had panted for so long and so hard that he was frothing at the mouth. "Oh, Oliver!" Eden hugged him tighter. Soon his breathing calmed, and he was his normal happy self. We hoped he would adjust.

He didn't.

Every time we tried the kennel, we came home to the crate on the other side of the room and a lather-soaked pup. The thought of him being so worked up that he thrust the crate into motion made us all sad.

It occurred to me there was one unconsecrated room left in the house—Eden's. Sometimes during the day, Oliver and Jack would rest on her bed. I suggested we try "kenneling" the two of them in Eden's room.

Thank God, Jack is easygoing. His relationship with Oliver had taken some time to develop, which had surprised us. From the time Jack was a puppy, he craved the company of dogs. He loved the park, his puppy kindergarten, even the vet—as long as he got to be with other dogs.

Whenever dogs came to visit, he was thrilled to play. Sure, he always let them know it was his house, but he was never overly territorial. In the early weeks after the fire, he was so happy at Dawn and Thom's, with all his canine cousins. We always assumed if we ever got a second dog, Jack would be thrilled.

When we brought Oliver home, we stopped at the boarder to pick up Jack. We thought it would be best for them to meet on neutral territory and asked the owner if we could introduce them there. Jack was a favorite of hers, and she was excited to meet Oliver.

She was the only one. Jack was wary from the start. It was like he knew this wasn't just any dog. It didn't help that Oliver was a little jerk and tried to establish dominance from the get-go.

"Doing his gentlemanly business" was Eden's euphemism, but "trying to"was more like it, since Oliver was about a quarter the size of Jack. Jack would be walking around, and Oliver would reach his front paws on Jack's back and then scuttle around on his back paws, trying to keep up. If Jack was lying down, Oliver would get right to it until Jack snapped at him to stop. This went on all day, every day, from the second we brought him home. Oliver's stud days were behind him, but he hadn't gotten the memo.

For weeks, Jack looked perplexed and slightly troubled.

Why is this guy still here? was as clear as if it was written in a thought bubble above Jack's head. He ignored Oliver—other than thwarting the ongoing assaults as necessary. But both dogs loved to lie in the patches of sunlight streaming through our French doors. Oliver cuddled up on the rug right by the door, and Jack lay several feet away. They quickly reached détente.

After a few weeks with us, Oliver calmed down, and Jack, ever an amiable soul, relaxed in his presence. Gradually the two dogs moved closer in every sense. During the day, they inched physically closer and closer until finally they were snuggled together. Though a Lab couldn't be more different from a pug physically, their shared blackness and cute faces made them look like a perfect match—two black dogs. Sometimes they would lie back to back; other times, Jack would be on his side and Oliver would cuddle up in the space between Jack's belly and legs. Once, I found Jack lying belly down, head on his front paws, while Oliver faced the opposite direction with his face smooshed into Jack's hip.

At night Oliver slept on Eden's bed, and Jack on our bedroom floor or one of his own beds, but during the day, they were inseparable. When I suggested "kenneling" them in Eden's room, it seemed a natural solution. The first time we tried, there was no hesitation. "Jack! Oliver!" Eden called them, and they ran right in. "Up! Up!" she urged, and Jack hopped right up. Oliver followed suit, and they settled in immediately.

When we returned, Eden ran right upstairs to check and found both dogs sleeping. We were delighted to have a solution. All was well for several months, until I noticed Eden's room was beginning to smell like a kennel. This was only fair, since that was what it had become. This wasn't tenable.

I finally remembered that Dawn and Thom had an enormous kennel in their basement for two of their big dogs.

"What if we bought an extra-large kennel for Oliver *and* Jack?" Everyone thought that was a good solution. I picked up a kennel one size up from the one recommended for dogs Jack's size. We hauled one of the dog beds inside it for Jack's comfort and hoped Oliver wouldn't make a mess. For convenience, we set it up in our large upstairs hall, just outside our bedrooms. Oliver always happily trotted into the kennel, and Jack was mostly agreeable. Occasionally he would run into Eden's bedroom and jump up on the bed, ignoring our calls. He would look to the side and feign deafness, but all it took was a firm command for him to come and quickly settle into the kennel with Oliver. It was a relief to come home to two happy dogs.

The problem remained what to do when we were home. We just weren't accustomed to having to keep an eye on a dog. For years, Jack had been no trouble. There were still occasional temptations he failed to overcome. Anyone who left peanut butter toast or a stick of butter too close to the counter shouldn't be surprised when he rose above the counter with the majesty of a whale cresting and the intensity of a shark lunging for its prey. Snap! And the toast or stick of butter was gone. But this was easily remedied: Everyone pushed these impossible temptations to the middle of the island, and Jack remained (mostly) a very good boy.

Oliver's bathroom habits continued to be iffy. He could go weeks at a time with no incident, and everyone would relax. But then, almost immediately, messes or puddles were found in unexpected places.

"OLIVER!" the shout would go up, and then, just as quickly, "EDEN!"

I found myself longing for Jet.

"Do you ever think about Jet?" I asked Eden one day, as casually as I could manage.

"Yes," she said and looked me right in the eye. She knew exactly what I was thinking. "But Oliver *needed* us."

Before we adopted Oliver, we had talked about going away for spring break. My mom offered to take care of Jack while we were away, and then Oliver, once he came into our home. At first, I hoped he would adjust, but as the weeks passed and he still wasn't reliable, we decided it would be too much to ask my mother, who was having back pain, to be continually cleaning up after him. Add to that, Torey's sister-in-law was flying in for a visit with her three-month-old and much-longed-for baby girl, and we decided to postpone any travel. We settled on a day trip to one of the little towns along Lake Michigan's shoreline. Since we were going to be gone the whole day, we decided to take Oliver with us.

"I feel sad that Jack is being left at home," Eden said when we were getting ready to leave, "He's the one who deserves to go, and he *loves* Lake Michigan."

This was true, but it's one thing to take a lapdog on a road trip and another thing altogether to take a big Labrador retriever.

"What do you think?" I asked Paul.

"I think he'd love to come."

"Well of course he would. Do you think it's foolish?"

"I think he should come."

As if he knew we were talking about him, Jack hopped up and walked to the back door. Riding in the backseat next to Christopher, his tail was wagging in obvious delight at being able to come along. It was a beautiful, sunny day. We had a nice drive and stopped at a park with beach access, where leashed dogs were allowed. The park was up on a wooded bluff. Although we couldn't see the lake, Jack could sense it was there, and he was so eager to get to it that he nearly dragged Paul down the trail.

Christopher and Paul took turns walking him, and he was thrilled to bury his face in the sand and run along the shore. If you've never been to the Great Lakes, they look just like the ocean, with long sandy beaches and water that stretches to the horizon. The only perceptible difference is there is no scent of salt in the air.

Oliver, who spent the first three years of his life in an outdoor cage and the fourth in a little house in the city, didn't know what to think. He refused to go near the water and pulled on his leash to stay as far away as possible. Eventually Eden cuddled with him on a log. Lydia and I walked together along the beach and then took a turn holding Oliver so Eden could walk the shore with Paul, Christopher, and Jack.

Oliver kept his eye on her, but he was happy to sit quietly with us—well, quietly for a pug. He sneezed and yawned widely and loudly, unfurling his long tongue before snapping his mouth shut, then licking his chops and sneezing again and starting the whole cycle over. Lydia and I looked at each other over his little head and smiled. Both of us were happy to listen to the water touch the shore, soak up the sun, and hug this ridiculous little dog we both had come to love so much.

It was so good to be outside, but even more, it was wonderful to be together as a family at one of our favorite places. The advent of spring is deeply cherished in Michigan after our long, hard winters, and it felt like we had finally weathered a winter of another kind.

After a bit, we went into town and had lunch at a café. It was warm enough to sit outside, and everyone who passed greeted the two dogs. "Look at the puppy!" more than one child shouted.

Jack was always good with kids, and we were happy to see Oliver was too. He sat at attention and received friendly pats in stride. Paul and I smiled.

"It seems like only yesterday it was these two"—Paul nodded toward Christopher and Lydia—"who were begging to pet a stranger's dog."

"I know. I can't believe it." Now it was our turn, and we were all glad to pay it forward with our two good dogs.

We made one last stop at the town's used bookstore. Wherever we travel, we always find the local bookstores, new or used. Before the fire, we owned thousands of books, and they were some of the first and only things we replaced in the early days and weeks. Looking back, I can see that my frequent trips into bookstores were some of the rare times my brain would try to process losing all my possessions. I had been able to let go of so much without a second glance, but the books were a peculiar loss. Before the fire, going to a bookstore meant browsing for something new, but after the fire, it was yet another opportunity to mourn what had been lost. It always felt so strange to find a title and think, "I have that very edition"—only to realize, yet again, that I had once owned it but did no longer. Then, as I began to replace books, I couldn't remember what I had reacquired and what was still missing. Visiting a bookstore, which was once an unmitigated delight, became tinged with longing and sorrow, and I often felt this compulsion to explain to the bookseller why I needed what I was looking for.

Years later, when I read *The Little Bookstore of Big Stone Gap* by Wendy Welch, I recognized myself in a story about a customer who was searching for "a handful of fairly eclectic titles . . . By turns quiet and garrulous, she talked over me as I started to answer her questions, ignoring my answers. Truth be told, she seemed . . . odd."*

The customer was rude and demanding and snapped at Welch. Eventually she started to cry, and the whole story came out. She had lost everything including her three dogs in a house fire. Since Welch's bookstore is in the mountains of Virginia, forest fires are not uncommon, and this woman was the first of many such customers. Welch learned one of the first things a fire victim replaces is their favorite book from childhood. This woman sat with Welch and her husband for two hours, drinking tea and telling them everything. Welch says, "In all honesty, the scariest, hardest, saddest, most important stories found in a bookshop aren't in the books; they're in the customers."**

I was always polite to the booksellers I met, but I knew that overwhelming feeling of disorientation and profound grief, and I'm sure they, too, found me . . . odd.

But this day, in this bookstore, I was happy and at peace. Lydia chatted with one of the owners and bought a stack of books. Christopher struck up a nice conversation with one of the customers and befriended the two store dogs, both giant labradoodles. Eden kept our dogs and Paul company outside. I browsed happily through the children's books and then checked out fiction, looking for replacement copies of Pym and Wodehouse. (I eventually learned to start with these authors and go from there to prevent the sense of overwhelm.) I listened to Christopher and Lydia talking politely and intelligently and enjoyed being together but

---

*Wendy Welch, *The Little Bookstore of Big Stone Gap* (New York: St. Martin's Press, 2012), 134–35.
**Ibid., 141.

separate, and for the first time since the fire, I felt completely at home in a bookstore and didn't feel a need to explain our loss.

A few weeks later, I was sitting at my desk when I heard a siren and then saw a couple emergency vehicles drive by. I felt an immediate tightening in my chest. It wasn't always like that. There were times I could hear a siren and feel no stress, but many times I did, even if it was subtle.

I thought back to a time a year after the fire when Eden and I were walking into a store and an ambulance came racing down the road. The way the sound bounced off the corner of the building, it almost seemed like it was coming from inside. We both jumped and were scanning the area, looking for the danger and a way of escape. We were scared, almost panicked, until we heard the siren moving away and we understood what it was.

That was before trauma therapy and more than a year ago. This time, hearing the ambulance, I called to Eden in the living room with Oliver.

"Did the siren bother you?"

"Yes," she replied in a calm voice.

"You want a hug?" I asked.

"I'm OK," she said.

I looked out my window and watched the big ladder truck of our township's fire department turn the corner. I squinted to see if I could recognize some of the firefighters we have gotten to know, but it was too far away and the truck was moving fast.

"Do you want to pray for whomever is having the emergency?" I asked.

This has been a practice of mine with the children since Christopher and Lydia were very young, long before Eden was born. It became a reflex for all of us whenever we heard a siren of any sort, but I had fallen out of the habit since the fire.

"I already did," Eden said.

"Good girl," I said and then bowed my head. I was glad to be in this part of the healing—still hearing and feeling the alarm but once again thinking of and praying for others.

nineteen

After

Summer came and went, and it was time for Eden to go back to school. After a year of school at home, she was ready to return to public school for fourth grade. The only question was where. The school she attended for her Mandarin Immersion program wasn't close to our house. Since we don't live in a subdivision, she had never had neighborhood friends. Her local, assigned school was bigger, and she wouldn't know anyone. Taking everything into account, we asked for permission to attend another elementary school within our district, where she had a kind friend she had met playing basketball. I would have to drive her there and back, but it seemed more than worth it for what we were all hopeful would be a good and fresh start back to school.

That first morning, she got up early with Christopher and Lydia; she couldn't wait to begin her day. The dogs were both up and about, feeling the change in the air. "Do you want to take Eden to school?" I asked when it was time to leave. They scurried out the door.

At school, Eden hopped out of the van. "Bye, Mama! Bye, Jackie! Bye, Oliver!" she called out cheerfully, and then she was gone. I always cry on the first day of school, and this year I wasn't alone. Oliver ran to the back of the van and stood up on his hind legs. He stared out the window, whining loudly as he watched Eden disappear into the school.

I pulled out of the parking lot, but the whining continued. "Come on, Ollie," I called back. "I know just how you feel."

He climbed up and sat on my lap the whole way home.

All day long, he was unsettled. He was accustomed to Eden leaving from time to time, but it was as if he could sense this was something new and wrong. I had a big project I was working on, and I was counting on the next couple weeks to knuckle down while the kids were in school but had not taken the dogs into account. All day long, I was up and down, opening the door for them. This was a normal routine of Jack's, and Oliver was happy to follow his lead. When he wasn't outside tagging along after Jack or sunning on the deck, he was right by my side. He didn't know where his girl was, and he wasn't letting me out of his sight.

Finally it was time. "Who wants to get Eden?" Both dogs ran for the back door. And thus we began a daily practice. Every day when it was time to pick up Eden from school, both dogs scuttled into the van. Jack always settled onto the backseat, sitting sideways, looking out the window the entire trip, placid and silent. Oliver often perched in front of Jack, faced forward. As soon as we arrived at Eden's school, he hopped onto the passenger seat and pressed against the window, watching for his girl. It was never long before he began to whine in contractions, a distress call that kept growing louder and louder. Just when he and I couldn't take any more, Eden came running, and Oliver exploded in joyful barking. Every single day.

A few weeks after school started, Paul was working from home and needed to run an errand. The dogs saw him gathering his things and ran to the back door.

"Where do you think you're going?" Paul asked as he looked down into the dogs' upturned faces.

"They love to take a ride," I said.

Paul opened the door. "OK, guys. Who wants to go with me?" Both dogs came running. They sat quietly in the backseat while Paul ran his errands. On the way home, they were stopped at a light when Oliver began his signature goat-like groaning. Paul was surprised. They were nowhere near Eden's school, and it was early.

Oliver hopped up into the passenger seat, whining and crying nonstop. Paul looked out and realized they were stopped behind a school bus and began to laugh. Oliver knew a school bus meant Eden was near.

"Oh, Oliver!" Eden said that evening when Paul told the story. Oliver leaned into her, chin up, eyes shut, completely content.

It was a good back-to-school for all the children. Fall faded into winter, and soon we were preparing for Christmas—our first with two dogs—and, unbelievably, our second since we had moved into the new house.

One morning, I woke up in the wee hours and got up to get a drink of water. Jack, who had been sleeping on the floor at the foot of our bed, got up too and followed me down the hall. I always like walking down the stairs with him. He keeps pace with me, and it's sweet to see how he holds back in order to stay by my side. On the last step from the bottom, I stopped at the window and turned my head to look out into the darkness and caught the smallest glint of light. A car was coming over the hill, and its headlights illuminated the ice-covered branches of a large oak tree hanging over the road and seemed to frame the scene. As I watched, the lights came closer, the brightness growing and widening, shining through the glittering ice. Jack stood on the step beneath me waiting, silent. It was unutterably beautiful.

I thought of the morning of the fire and another pair of headlights shining as we stood waiting. Fire and ice, darkness and light.

At the old house, I never looked out the window when I awoke in the night. Was the only reason I was here to witness this beautiful moment because an arsonist had set my house on fire? What else am I able to see that, without suffering, I would have otherwise overlooked? And what is happening all around me that I don't notice, that I'm looking past and just miss? C. S. Lewis said that pain is God's "megaphone to rouse a deaf world."* Could it also be its microscope?

The car paused at the stop sign, turned right, and drove west into the darkness.

That spring, I felt the first stirrings of anticipation. I began to take a look at the gardens again with interest and excitement. In the fall, Eden and I had planted bulbs, and nearly every morning, I walked around the house inspecting the beds, looking for what was pushing through the soil. Both dogs were happy to follow me on my rounds, and I enjoyed having them with me. It was a long-awaited pleasure to have not just one but two dogs ambling by my side.

When Jack was a puppy, we had to keep him on a leash or in the fenced-in part of the yard. If anyone left the gate open, Jack frequently made a dash for the neighbor's yard or, less often, ran across the road. More than once that first chaotic year, I got a call from a kindly person

*C. S. Lewis, *The Problem of Pain* (1940; repr., New York: Macmillan, 1962), 93.

who had Jack by the collar, his tail wagging to beat the band. I was always equally grateful and embarrassed to have lost him, but Jack's rescuers were happy to help and relieved he hadn't gotten hurt.

As Jack grew up, these adventures were far less common, but every year or so, the gate would get left open, and he would go on a walkabout. The first week we had Oliver, he dashed up the hill to visit the neighbors, but after that, he never strayed far from the house, let alone the yard. If Eden was home, he was right by her side, but when she was away, he could be tempted outside and was Jack's little shadow. They loved to wander around the yard or lounge in the sun. The back porch was a favorite spot, as was the driveway. One day, I couldn't see them in any of their usual haunts, and when I called them in, they didn't immediately come running.

Occasionally Jack ignored me, but not Oliver, although Eden was away visiting a friend—so all bets were off.

I walked around the house and checked the garage. There was no sign of them.

"Christopher!" I yelled upstairs.

"Yeah, Mom?"

"The boys are missing. Will you come with me to find them?"

"Sure."

The few times Jack went missing, it was almost always to visit our neighbors, who lived over a hill and through the woods behind our house. Usually we just walked up there, but because Oliver was with Jack, I felt a sense of urgency. To save time I jumped in the van, and we got to the neighbor's place in less than a minute. There was no sign of the dogs, and our neighbors weren't home.

"Let's walk around the house," I said to Christopher. He went one way; I went the other; and we met in the middle—no dogs.

Our next-door neighbor was up another hill. This was where Oliver wandered that first week. I was hopeful, but the dogs weren't there either. I asked my neighbor to call if they turned up.

I decided to head east—the direction we most commonly take on our walks. As I drove, I kept my eye on the walking path, willing two black dogs to appear. They were so clear in my mind—Jack merrily trotting and Oliver scampering behind him—but they were nowhere to be seen.

I was beginning to panic. I turned around and drove west and then north up the other way for several miles.

"Are you worried we aren't going to find them?" Christopher asked.

"Yeah. I'm trying not to think about that, but I'm worried. Please pray."

"OK, Mom, I can do that." He shut his eyes tight.

I thought about Eden. That ridiculous dog was a pain in the neck, but he was Eden's heart, and despite everything, I adored him too. What would we do without Oliver? I couldn't bear to think what that would do to Eden to lose her beloved pup. What could we even say?

I got a call from a number I didn't recognize and let it go. The caller left a message, which I then listened to. It was a woman's voice.

"Hi, are you missing a black Lab?" Jack? "He's here at my house. Call me." She left her number, but I was already returning it.

"Hello."

"Hi! I'm calling about the black Lab. He's mine. Is there a pug with him? A little black pug?"

"Yeah, there's a pug too. They came out of the woods into my back yard. The Lab came right into my house when I opened the door, but the pug is sitting in the front yard."

Oh, Jack! Oh, Oliver! I could just see Jack—who had ever relied on the kindness of strangers—barreling his way into someone's house, and poor little Oliver holding back, uncertain and afraid.

She gave me her address. It was about a half mile from our house. I was there in a minute.

Oliver was sitting in the middle of the lawn, staring at the house. As soon as he saw me, though, he came running. I picked him up, and he sneezed in my face. I didn't even care and hugged him tight. I was so relieved. I had been desperate to find him, thinking only of Eden, but the joy I felt now was purely my own in having him back again.

The front door opened, and Jack came bounding out. Christopher hustled him into the van.

The woman was a dog lover and happy to help.

"I tried to get the little one to come in the house, but he wouldn't budge." This didn't surprise me. I could imagine Jack taking off, and

Oliver following him with the thought of finding his girl—only to find himself so far from home. I thanked her profusely. I was so grateful for her kindness and concern. Some people would have been annoyed or alarmed if two strange dogs showed up, but her first thought was to help.

I have often rolled my eyes when I heard, what sounded to my ears, the cheesy phrase "being the hands and feet of Jesus," but after spending so much time looking for the presence of God and meditating on the idea and reality of him being "with us," I was beginning to wonder if his chosen way to live among us is most often through us. What if loving others as ourselves, in large and small ways, is a key part of how God reveals himself? It seems like a bad plan. We're so fallible. We so often let each other down. But what if that's the way it really works?

As I pulled into our driveway, I saw a pair of Eden's sandals on the front porch next to a metal pail she uses for picking flowers. In the front yard, Christopher's bike was lying on its side. I stopped the van and looked at the beautiful house, the sight of which for months had left me cold, and felt a great surging of love and a profound feeling of home. Home was where my little girl's sandals were and where my boy's bike was tossed. I thought of Lydia's colorful hats and jackets, hanging neatly in the mudroom, which I loved to catch glimpses of whenever I passed. I thought of the way my heart lifted when I heard tires on the gravel and looked out the window and saw Paul's truck pulling into the garage. "Home is wherever I'm with you" went the chorus in a song I had been singing for months. And it was true.

"When did you become a crazy dog lady?" Torey asked one day out of the blue.

"What do you mean?"

"Every time I turn around, you're posting another picture of your dogs on Facebook."

"I haven't posted anything in over a week."

"OK, I doubt that, and just the other day when you wanted to show me a picture of Eden, you had to scroll through at least thirty pictures of dogs to get to it—and even then, she was holding Oliver."

"Well, they're inseparable. I can't help that. Have you considered I spend more time with the dogs? If my children sat around all day posing adorably together, I would take more pictures of them."

Torey rolled her eyes.

Was I a crazy dog lady? Had it really come to that?

A few days later, I walked into my bathroom, and there was Oliver, sitting in the bottom of my enormous claw-foot tub. Eden was in the separate shower. This was not an unusual occurrence. Eden preferred to use our bathroom rather than the one she shared with Christopher and Lydia, and Oliver goes wherever she goes. One day, she decided to make a little bed for him on a folded towel in the bottom of the tub. Since then, there he would sit or lie, perfectly content.

When we were building our house, I had decided against a tub in the master bath and relished the thought of saving money in the short term and cleaning in the long term, but then Paul—who had less than a handful of requests when it came to the entire house—asked for a tub big enough to have a relaxing soak with me. As delightful as it sounded, I pointed out we rarely took baths.

"What if we try something new?" he asked.

He persisted—and how could I refuse? I preferred the look of a free-standing tub rather than the immense soaker ones and had to scour the nation to find a claw-foot big enough to bathe a giant. I finally tracked one down in Florida. A crane hauled it up to the second floor, and the house was built around it. In the two years since we moved in, Paul and I had bathed in it once.

I had taken a few baths on my own, but every time I looked at the tub, I had the same litany of thoughts. *If only we hadn't bought it, we would have saved so much money, and I wouldn't have to clean it, and our bathroom would have been smaller, and our bedroom could have been bigger, and*—and . . . and . . . oh, the perseverating ruts. The first time I walked in and saw Oliver sitting there, I was too surprised to think anything.

"What is your pug doing in my tub?" I asked Eden.

"I didn't want him to have to sit on the cold tile, so I made him a little bed."

I looked at that little dog, his tail curled and unfurled in a sort of wag, his tongue stuck out, his head up, his eyes open wide, staring right back at me.

"This is ridiculous."

"It's his babysitter, Mama!"

I bent over the tub to get close to the pug. He stared up at me and blinked.

"Oliver," I said, "what are you doing in my tub?"

He opened his mouth wide; his long tongue stuck out for a moment; and then he snapped his jaw shut and sneezed.

"Oliver!" I picked him up and held him close. His little paws rested on each of my shoulders. He breathed in that strangled little wheeze of his. I rubbed my cheek against his velvety ear and kissed the top of his head.

In that moment, I wasn't bemoaning the billion dollars we had spent on that rarely used tub. The thought occurred to me: *What if I let myself off the hook? Just let it go? The money is long spent. What if I just enjoy the tub? What if I just enjoy everything? What if I—as silly as it sounds—forgive myself for all the mistakes I have made?* It was something to consider. From that day on, whenever I walked into my bathroom, I no longer reflexively regretted the tub. Most often, I pictured Ollie and smiled. Maybe I *was* a crazy dog lady, but there were worse things to be.

For Father's Day, Paul wanted to eat at home and relax by the pool. It was just the five of us and the dogs. Although he never wants to get in the water, Jack loves being by the pool with us. When we visit a lake, we can't get him out of the water, but the pool makes him nervous. We think it's because our pool only has ladders, and we suppose he doesn't like not being able to climb out on his own.

He loves to play catch. We have a favorite game where we throw the ball to the top of the slide. Jack stands beside it and tries to grab the ball before it falls back into the water. Even with his overbite, he's surprisingly successful. Everyone roots for him and cheers when he catches it. Invariably he gets so excited that he starts running around the pool until he collapses.

Oliver is less of a fan. We have to be careful because pugs overheat so easily. On scorching days, he can't be outside. Because he doesn't like being away from Eden, we put him in my mother's little house, which overlooks the pool, and he happily takes a nap. Win-win.

Father's Day was perfect—warm enough that a swim felt refreshing, but not so hot it was uncomfortable for humans or unsafe for brachycephalic dogs. Lydia and I were lounging and reading; Christopher was lying on a float in the deep end, eyes shut, his face upraised. Paul and Eden were swimming around and chatting in the shallow end. Jack was sitting in his favorite shaded spot in front of the pool shed, and Oliver was under my lounge chair. Eden swam to the edge of the pool.

"Oliver," she called.

He ignored her.

"Oliver, come here!" This time, it was a command.

He crawled out from under my chair and slowly walked to the edge of the pool. Eden picked him up and put him over her shoulder—one of his favorite positions. Both little paws clutched her neck. Oliver was obviously nervous, but he didn't fight. You could see his conflict—being held by his girl versus being in the deep water. He was perfectly safe. Even if Eden dropped him, he can swim and so many of us were around to grab him if necessary. He didn't know that, and so he didn't feel safe. Regardless, he was with Eden, so he held on tightly and didn't resist. More than anything, he wanted to be with her.

Eden lowered them into the water, and Oliver pawed at her. Eden pulled him off and let go. He held his head above water, his eyes bulging more than usual. Breathing hard, he splashed his way toward the ladder. He looked desperate.

"Eden, either hold him or let him get out. He doesn't like it."

"Mama, he's fine. I'm right here. He's perfectly safe."

"*I* know that, but he doesn't."

"What if I got a float?"

"You can try."

She set Oliver on the side of the pool. He shook vigorously while she grabbed a baby float. She got back in the pool and picked him up. Then she carefully maneuvered his back legs into the mesh seat. Oliver was obviously nervous, but Eden stayed close and spoke reassuringly to him. He eventually relaxed and slowly blinked.

"He likes it!"

"I'd say he tolerates it." But I was smiling. "Why don't you set him free?"

Eden pushed the float to the edge of the pool and helped Oliver out. He shook hard and trotted toward my chaise.

"Come here, Ollie!" I pulled him up onto my lap and wrapped him in a towel. He nestled in beside me and turned to keep an eye on Eden.

It felt good to be outside, to enjoy our home and each other, and it was such a beautiful day. I looked up to see the plain, almost austere white of the house, with its simple roofline pointing like an arrow toward the blue and cloudless sky. The lawns rolled in and out of shadows, still the deep and verdant green of early summer. Birds flew and called. If someone who knew nothing about us saw this scene, they might imagine we lived an idyllic life. In many ways we did, and still, in a couple weeks, it would be the third anniversary of the fire.

We want everything tied up in neatly bundled packages, but that so rarely happens. Life can't always be simplified into easy formulas. I was grateful for our house, but it was never going to be the happy ending to this story.

I thought about Eden and Oliver and their sweet relationship, which is like something out of a book. And yet, depending on how the story is told, where the focus is placed, it could look like both of them had had hard lives.

Is it a sad story or a happy one? We want to know before we buy the book.

Was Oliver the pathetic little dog who spent three years of his life in a puppy mill or the happiest and most-beloved pup? Was Eden the sad victim of an arsonist or the plucky heroine of her own fairy tale?

It isn't an either-or. One story doesn't negate the other. It will always be both. And I was beginning to think the whole story is the richest.

twenty

And Then . . .

This is where I want to end this story. Let's leave it here, with all of us healthy and happy, finally enjoying our home, healed and loving life—you know, happily ever after.

The End

If we stop right now, I won't have to tell you about the car accident we got into a month later—the one where we landed upside down in the middle of a Canadian highway in the wee hours of the morning, resulting in the entire family rushed to the hospital in separate ambulances. For a couple of us, there would be concussions, head wounds, lots of stitches, and eventual surgeries to remove glass. One of us would have an arm dragged across the highway. This, too, would need lots of stitches and a subsequent surgery. All of us would get bumped and shaken and another whopping case of post-traumatic stress. I would get another massive insurance claim to file—this one, international.

And if I end the story now, I won't have to tell you about Oliver getting cancer.

Yeah, the pug got cancer.

I really don't want to tell you about that.

For Eden's twelfth birthday, she asked for and received an aquaponics fish tank. With her own money, she bought its tenant—a beautiful blue beta fish she named Mr. Peacock. Soon he was living the good life, swimming around miniatures of the Eiffel Tower and a British telephone box with radish and wheat grass sprouts growing above them all. Eden was delighted. Every morning, she carefully fed Mr. Peacock just enough but not too much—even when she was tempted to give him more.

There are those who claim that beta fish live forever. I've seen them in various offices, swimming on the receptionists' desks. I've been told, "We couldn't kill it if we tried." Alas, killing fish is a knack the Hodgsons seem to have, so I responded to Eden's joy with more than slight hesitation. Two weeks is the longest any of our fish have ever lived. Mr. Peacock made it just short of three.

He died on a Thursday. At bedtime when I went to tuck in Eden, I found her crying. I kneeled beside her and stroked her face.

"I'm so sorry, sweetheart. Mr. Peacock was a good fish."

"I know. I'm going to miss him so much, and that makes me think about what am I going to do when Oliver dies someday?"

I shuddered at the thought.

"Maybe I just love animals too much."

While it is true that some of us love intensely and unreservedly, who can quantify what is too much?

"Eden, today you do have Oliver. His death is not today's worry." I said this gently. "Tonight, and in the days to come, as you mourn Mr. Peacock, why don't you hold and cuddle Oliver, and thank God you have him."

We both looked at him. He had already fallen asleep, his head tucked under her arm, his face smooshed against her, snoring softly.

I continued to stroke Eden's forehead.

"We risk getting hurt anytime we love. And you *do* love animals, especially—with your whole heart. That's not wrong; it's just painful sometimes."

She yawned and nodded. I knew the best thing for her was sleep. We prayed, and I gave her a good-night kiss.

The very next day, I took Oliver to the vet for his annual checkup. Christopher was taking a gap year between high school and college and was working, but he had the day off, so he came along too. The routine examinations went well. Oliver was calm and quiet, but when it came time to trim his nails and aspirate a growth on his chest, they took him to the back, where he tended to do better for these sorts of procedures. Christopher and I could hear the alien-like shrieking that was his patented protest, but even those weren't as long and frequent as his first checkups. Our li'l guy was growing up.

After a bit, the technician returned with him in her arms. When she set him down, he made a beeline for our legs and settled on the floor underneath Christopher, panting.

"Were you able to take care of everything?" I asked.

"We're going to hold off on the nails until he has his dental work done. We can get those easily when he's sedated."

"Oh, Oliver!" We all looked at this pathetic little dog, and he stared back, unblinking, ears down and back—he had clearly been through the wringer—but his tail thumped in spite of himself.

"Doctor is going to take a look at the cells from the growth, and then she'll be right back."

We waited in silence. Neither of us liked the sound of that.

When the doctor returned to the room, her face was neutral, but I knew something was wrong.

"There's something that looks a little concerning."

This is exactly what you never want any sort of medical person to say. Ever.

She got right to it: There were mast cells. It didn't look good, and she recommended immediate removal. As luck would have it, they had an opening first thing on Monday morning. "Does that work for you?"

"Yes," I said.

She nodded as if to move on, but I didn't really understand what she was saying. I could see possibilities, but I wanted to be clear.

"Wait. Would you level with me? What are you saying? Are you saying he has cancer?"

"Not necessarily. I don't know if it's a tumor. I've had it where a mass looked bad, and then I went in to remove it and it was a lipoma."

"OK. So that's the best-case scenario?"

"Yes."

"But this doesn't look like a lipoma?"

"No."

"What if it is a tumor?"

"We'll try to get all of it, and then we'll send it in to be tested."

"To see whether it's benign or malignant?"

"Yes, and if it's malignant, we'll learn the grade. I'm going to get you some information so you can read up this weekend."

I started to cry.

"I'm sorry," she said.

When we got back in the van, Christopher held Oliver in his lap.

"Did you understand what the vet said?" I asked.

"Yeah, I understood. Oliver may have cancer."

"We just have to pray he'll be OK. Let's do that right now."

I grabbed his hand and prayed as we drove home.

When Paul returned from work, I collapsed into his arms. He held me close. Christopher came behind me and pulled Paul into a group hug.

I couldn't stop crying. I knew I had to pull it together for Eden's sake, but it felt like the world was tilting and Oliver was slipping away. Darkness was at the margins of everything.

Oliver had been such a catalyst in Eden's—in our—healing. We couldn't lose him now.

At least we wouldn't have to tell Eden right away. She was having a sleepover with her cousins. Knowing I had another day brought some small measure of comfort, but there was no question we had to tell her. Oliver was her dog, and she had every right to know and pray for him. I thought of how she would respond if he got sick—or, God forbid, if he died in surgery, without having had a chance to pray for him and give him special attention. I asked Paul if he would give her the news.

"I just think you will be able to say it without breaking down."

"I'll tell her," he said in that calm and steady tone I was counting on.

I opened one of my favorite books on prayer and then another about essential oils. I prayed and liberally anointed him, then read through the papers from the vet. I was going to have *all* my bases covered.

The phone rang. It was my sister, Torey, the host for Eden's sleepover that night. "Your baby is being weird."

"What do you mean?"

"She's lying on my sofa because she says she's having trouble walking."

"What! Did she fall off the sled?"

"No. She said nothing happened. She just had to lie down suddenly."

"Let me talk to her." Torey handed the phone to Eden.

"Hi, Mama."

"So what's going on?"

"I don't know. I don't feel good."

"Did something happen?"

"No. I was fine, and then all of a sudden, I felt like I couldn't stand up. You know that feeling where your knees don't work?"

"No. I've never had that. Do you want to stay, or should we come get you?"

"I want to stay, but I think I should probably come home."

I sighed. I wasn't feeling brave enough to see her yet. "OK, Daddy and I will be right there."

We brought Oliver along, and he scampered right over to Eden on the sofa as soon as Torey opened the door.

"Ugh, he stinks! Why did you put oils on him?"

There was no good way to answer this. "Because I wanted him to smell good for Aunt Torey. You know how picky she is." This wasn't a complete lie. Torey loves both our dogs, but she never hesitates to let us know when they're smelly.

"Now *I* think he stinks!"

"How are you feeling?" I changed the subject.

"Fine. I just felt like I couldn't walk."

This was troubling. On the drive over, I realized her leg trouble began during, or soon after, Oliver's appointment. What could it mean that she had been literally brought to her knees upon his diagnosis being uttered, even without her knowing? It couldn't be good.

I pulled Torey aside and told her what was going on and started to cry again.

"I just don't know what we'll do if something happens to that dog. What will happen to Eden?"

"I'm so sorry," Torey said. "We'll pray. Let me know when I can tell the girls."

On the way home, Oliver sat on Eden's lap.

"Mama, why did you put so many oils on Oliver? I'm really mad at you."

There was no avoiding it now.

"Eden, I'm concerned about him. At his appointment today, the vet said we need to have the lump on his chest removed—" I had to pause as a lump in my own throat made speaking impossible. I squeezed Paul's hand.

"You know how we thought it was a just a ball of fat?" he said. "It may be something more serious than that, and the vet wants to remove it to make sure, so he's going to have the procedure Monday morning."

"If it's not fat, what could it be?" Eden asked.

"It could be a tumor," Paul said without a hint of fear or horror.

I had been breathing deeply and praying. I tried to keep my voice upbeat. "So we just need to pray for Oliver and hope for the very best." I was glad she couldn't see the tears streaming down my face.

There was a moment of silence.

"I think he's going to be fine," Eden said. "God's brought him this far; I don't think a little tumor is going to get him."

Her tone was calm and absolutely certain.

Little tumors get people and animals all the time, I thought. *Do you understand it could be cancer and that Ollie could DIE?* I wanted to ask, but I knew I needed to keep my thoughts—and my anxieties—to myself. I felt like we were on the edge of a canyon. What would we do if this little dog died?

"Do you think she really understands?" I asked Paul after Eden went to bed.

"I think she does."

"She was so certain he's going to be fine. I'm not sure she understands what he's up against."

"I just think she's clear—that's not his story."

"Dying an early death from cancer?"

"Yeah."

I emailed family and friends and asked them to pray. After a slight hesitation, I contacted the church's prayer chain and put in a request there too.

That night I lay awake in bed. *Could Outrageous Oliver really die?* Of course, I knew he could, but in a way, I couldn't truly believe it. After everything he and Eden had been through, and knowing how important he is to her, it would be beyond heartbreaking; it would be cruel.

I slept terribly. I woke frequently—and every time, it was with this sinking uncertainty about Oliver and then Eden. My chest ached. I couldn't get on top of the worry.

I prayed incessantly. I found myself trying to coach God. "I'm so thankful you gave Eden Oliver, and we both know how healing he has been for her. She ADORES him, and—despite everything—so do the rest of us, and I just think it would look REALLY bad for you, not to mention BREAK MY BABY'S HEART, and maybe DESTROY HER FAITH if he dies of cancer a MERE THREE YEARS after we got him. But Thy will be done. HEAL THE PUG. HEAL THE PUG. OH, PLEASE! OH, PLEASE! HEAL OLIVER."

Friends wrote and called to ask how we were doing and to say they were praying.

I told everyone about Eden's peace and indefatigable faith. I didn't need to explain how that made things for me. They all understood her heart was on the line.

"As you can imagine, my prayers have gotten more than a little bit all-cappy."

"Oh, Alison, I just love you and your all-caps prayers," one friend said, "And I join you in them."

All weekend long, I leaked tears. I wanted to be strong for Eden, calm and trusting, but the thought of life without Oliver would pass through my mind, and I would start to cry. Again.

"Why are you crying, Mama?" Eden asked.

"I'm sorry, honey. I'm really concerned about Oliver." *And* you! I thought. *I'm so worried for you and your precious heart.*

"He's going to be fine, Mama. I know he is," she said every single time.

Eden had a day off from school the morning of Oliver's surgery. She slept in so Oliver would too, and I woke her up just a few minutes before it was time to leave. The morning was bitterly cold, and Oliver shivered on Eden's lap as we drove to the vet. She pulled her coat around him and held him close.

At the vet's, the receptionist was especially upbeat and kind. *Has she read his chart? Does she* know *he isn't going to be OK?* I wondered. And then I remembered that everyone at our vet's office is caring and kind and understands the feelings people feel when their beloved pets need surgery. Even if there was no grave cause, it's normal to be concerned. And I had bawled all over her just two days before when I scheduled this appointment. There was that.

She led us into one of the examination rooms, and while we waited for the doctor, we took pictures and played with Oliver. He was happy and curious, per usual. Snuffling around and smelling the perimeter of the room, he plopped on his bum, his little pig tail curling and unfurling in its happy, puggy wag.

The vet entered and got right down on her knees.

"How's Oliver today?" she asked in the high-pitched, enthusiastic way most of us talk to animals, petting and stroking him. He stayed calm, relaxing into her hands, and she began a subtle examination that brought her to the mass on his chest.

"OK, here it is," she said to Eden and me. "We're going to take care of that!" She reverted to her dog voice and addressed Oliver, "Aren't we?"

He was now almost stretched out on the floor, but his eyes were wide-open, uneasy.

"There's also the bump on his paw," Eden said.

"Yes, I was going to take a look at that." The vet gently prodded Oliver's right paw. "We'll take good care of him. He's going to get a lot of attention today. Everyone loves a pug."

"They're special little dogs," I agreed.

We both kissed Oliver one more time.

"Bye-bye, sweetie," Eden said calm and strong.

Tears welled up in my eyes yet again.

"He's going to be fine, Mama," Eden said with complete certainty. I prayed she was right.

twenty-one

All-Cappy Prayers

They said they would call when Oliver was out of surgery, and again when he was waking up. I knew this. They were very courteous, and they understood—even with routine procedures—that owners are concerned and want to know what's going on every step of the way. Hours passed, and no word. Finally, when I just couldn't wait any longer, I called. When the receptionist answered, I tried to stay calm. "Hi, this is Alison, Oliver's owner. I just wanted to know how he's doing."

"Let me check. I know they just wrapped up today's surgeries. I'll be right back." I waited, worry mounting. "OK, I just spoke with Dr. V., and she said things went well. It did take a bit longer than expected, and she would like to keep him until six just to make sure he's awake. She'll talk to you then."

I wanted to ask, *Does she think he has CANCER?* but knew I had to wait. I hated that the surgery took longer than expected. I also noticed the vet hadn't said it looked like or was a lipoma. What someone doesn't say is as important as what they do. I hated it, but we would just have to wait until six o'clock. I called Paul to tell him and to ask him to come with us. Whatever the news, I didn't want to be alone with Eden when we heard.

We arrived right on time and waited in one of the examining rooms. I knew the receptionist had to know, but I made myself resist pumping her for information. I watched her demeanor, which seemed suspiciously cheery.

"I've got some release papers for you to look over." We took a look. Paul and Eden chatted politely, but I had no small talk in me. I sat quietly, my heart pounding in my chest. I felt like I was in the dock, awaiting my sentence.

Finally the doctor came in. She was to the point. She removed the growth on Oliver's chest. It came off fairly easily, and she was confident she had gotten all of it, with good margins. The lump in the paw was more problematic. It was entwined with the muscle and tendons, and she had to take great care and tried to get everything she could.

"Were they tumors?" I asked—although I felt I already knew the answer.

She nodded. "They were both mast cell tumors."

"Did they look cancerous?"

"Mast cells are a form of cancer."

My heart sank. She had sent the tumors to the lab and would hear back in five to seven days. She asked if we understood the care instructions. We did. She explained about the drain on Oliver's chest. We would need to clean it twice a day, and she recommended we find a toddler shirt for him to wear.

"Do you have any old T-shirts he could use?" she asked Eden.

Eden shook her head. "My shirts would be huge on him."

"You don't have any from when you were little—well, I guess you probably lost all that in the fire."

I typically don't expect people to remember. The lump in my throat grew. I looked at her and nodded. "We'll pick up a shirt for him."

"Probably about a 2T," she said. She went in the back to get Oliver.

When the doctor brought him in, the first thing I noticed was his bandaged paw hanging limply. His eyes were dull; he looked tired; and his tongue stuck out a little too far, even for a pug. I have a weak stomach and tried to ignore his shaved chest with the small tube sticking out the end of the neatly stitched wound. Eden would normally be the first to step up and hold him, but she stayed back with me. I looked at Paul, and he reached out to take Oliver and pulled him close.

The vet gave instructions. We would need to protect his paw and keep the bandage dry with a plastic baggie before he went outside, and— she stepped in the back to grab something—he would need to wear the cone of shame. She fastened it on him and then went over his medications. His first dose was to begin at 10:00 p.m.

On the way out to the car, Eden said, "I'd like you to drive so Daddy can keep holding Oliver." She opened the door for her dad and buckled him in with Oliver.

"I just need to stretch it as if you were a very fat man." She seemed herself and utterly unfazed by the diagnosis. I felt better just knowing what we were up against. We had a week to pray.

"How are you doing, honey?" I asked as I pulled out of the parking lot.

"I—" Eden's voice cracked, "I'm not sure."

"What are you thinking, Eden?"

"I was fine, but now I'm scared of his stitches and that drain."

"I am too," I said. "Will you clean the incision?" I asked Paul.

"I can do that," he said.

We stopped at a store to pick up supplies, and Paul waited in the van. Oliver was too tired to protest Eden's absence.

Once home, Oliver was woozy and out of sorts. We immediately put him in the little shirt we had bought, a bright blue T-shirt that proclaimed, "Big Brother." He staggered over to the big dog bed by our fireplace and whined until Eden came and curled up with him. He snuggled up next to her and snoozed. She was exhausted but refused to go to bed until he'd been given his first dose of medicine. By the time we got them in bed, it was after eleven.

Tucking them in took some doing. Oliver wanted to be right beside Eden. He was a notorious bed hog anyway, but with the cone whacking against her and his horrendous surgery breath and the seeping incision, Eden was miserable and repulsed. She was so tired that she rolled over and buried her face in her pillow. As I tiptoed out of the room, I figured they would be out for the night.

A few minutes later, I heard Eden's soft call. "Mama?"

When I opened the door, Oliver was sitting up and Eden was on her back, covers tossed aside.

"As soon as you left, he got up and started whining."

He was silent now, his little coned head cocked to the side, staring. Oh, Oliver.

"Honey, he's exhausted and drugged. He's probably uncomfortable and doesn't understand anything that's going on.

"I'm just so tired, Mama!"

"I know you are. If I thought he would stay with us, I'd take him to our room, but he wants to be with you."

"I don't want him. I'm sick of his whining."

"I understand," I said, thinking of my own bed.

I was tired too, but I wasn't angry or frustrated. It was one of those rare times I was able to be the kind of mother I always hoped to be.

"It's hard because he needs you, and you don't have anything left to give, do you?"

"No!"

I turned to the dog. "OK, Ollie. Let's get you resettled." I gently pushed him down and closer to the wall and pulled up the quilt over Eden. I covered Oliver with his little blanket and kissed them both, praying silently all the while.

"Sweet dreams, angel."

"Good night, Mama."

I wish I could say that was it, but we repeated this several times before Oliver finally fell asleep for the night.

The first full day was a busy one. I had to keep a close eye on him and carried him up and down the stairs. In order for him to eat, he had to have his cone off, and to go out, he needed a plastic baggy wrapped around his paw. When he came back in, it was baggy off, cone on. He wasn't entirely steady on his feet, and the vet warned about him tearing his sutures, so I was gingerly picking him up and setting him down all day long.

When Eden walked in the door after school, she made a beeline for Oliver.

"What's that bump on his head?" she asked.

"What bump?" I looked, and there—just to the right of center on his head—was a large protuberance about the size and shape of a Kraft caramel. It had not been there that morning, and I hadn't noticed it during the day. I called the vet and told the receptionist about it. She put me on hold to check in with the vet.

Could a tumor form so quickly? I couldn't bring myself to ask.

The receptionist returned. "The doctor says she would like to take a look. Unfortunately I don't have any appointments this afternoon, but we could get you in tomorrow morning at ten. Does that work?"

It did.

I was worried. It couldn't be good to see a strange bump spring up out of nowhere on your dog that had just had two tumors removed. That could not be good at all. I didn't say anything to Eden, and she didn't press it. I was taking Oliver in to the vet the next day. That seemed to be good enough for her.

But that night as I was tucking her in, she began to sob.

"I *knew* it was a lipoma," she said, "but I was wrong." This was it, the moment I had been dreading.

"You thought it was a lipoma, and you thought Oliver was going to be fine." I paused. I needed to be careful. "Just because it isn't a lipoma doesn't mean he's not going to be fine. Let's pray for him."

She shut her eyes tight and prayed silently, and I did too.

The next morning before she left for school, she asked me to call her after I went to the vet.

"Why?" I asked. If it was bad news, I didn't want to call her at school and disrupt her day.

"I want to know. Call me if it's good news."

I knew I had to call her, regardless. To not call her with bad news was to tell her and then make her wait to hear for sure.

The day was bitterly cold. I coaxed Oliver into his little dog bed and covered him with his special blanket. When we got to the office, I picked the whole thing up and carried it in. I knew we looked silly, but it was an easy way to keep him warm and safe and avoid putting pressure on his incision.

The vet came in right away and examined the bump.

"We're going to aspirate it, and then I'll take a look at the cells to see what we have." She whisked Oliver to the back. I prayed beggy, desperate, and all-cappy prayers while I waited.

When the vet returned with Oliver, the lump was gone, and the top of his head was shorn. He looked like a tiny monk.

"It wasn't a mast cell tumor," she said. "It was just a skin infection."

I exhaled audibly. Thank God. I squinted back tears. Thank God. Thank God. Thank God.

"Could a mast cell tumor have formed that quickly?"

"Yes, it could." She said it matter-of-factly, but something in the way she spoke told me she had been dreading it as much as I had.

On the way home, I called Eden's school and left a message for the secretary, asking her to tell Eden the good news. After days of dread, it felt so good to have anything positive to report.

That night, I called a wise and loving friend whose life is marked by prayer. I told her what was going on and asked her to pray. She was happy to oblige, and she prayed for me and my family with eloquence and great wisdom, but she came to the end of her prayer without remembering to pray for Oliver.

"Please pray the dog lives," I said.

"Oh, yes—Oliver!" And then she prayed with beauty and passion that Oliver would be healed and given a long and healthy life.

That night, I slept well and woke with a feeling of peace. The dread was gone, at least temporarily. I knew things still didn't look good for Oliver, but I had peace that we were going to make it through whatever *it* was.

Oliver's appointment to remove the drain was that morning. I coaxed him into his bed, tucked his blanket around his entire body, and placed him in the front passenger seat to drive to the animal hospital. It was bitterly cold again, but the sun was shining. Oliver sat beside me, placidly blinking. It was good to be with him. The weight that had been on my chest all week was gone, and I was so thankful for the reprieve. I reached over to pet Oliver's head, and he lifted his chin to lean into my caress.

Perhaps this is the secret to everything. I used to think that faith or trust is the absence of fear or the absence of the feelings of stress. But I think it's just feeling the feelings and continuing to move forward, or getting stuck sometimes and praying our all-cappy prayers. Sometimes we slump against counters and cry. Sometimes we feel the pain in our chests. And then we pet the dog, who may or may not be dying, and we call the friends who will listen, and we ask them to pray the dog will live, and we thank God he's alive today.

The vet took a look at Oliver's head. "That's starting to heal," she said.

"I'm so thankful it wasn't a tumor. I don't know what we would have done—any of us—but Eden especially." I was quiet for a moment while she continued her examination of Oliver. "Do you remember that I'm writing a book—and this dog is sort of the happy ending?"

"I remember," she said. She removed the drain quickly before Oliver was able to put up a fight. The bandage on his paw was another story. He began to struggle, backing into the technician, and then, as she adjusted her grasp, he thrust himself forward, knocking her off balance. After a few readjustments, she got a strong hold on him, and the vet snipped the bandage, pulled Oliver's paw free, and then set him on the ground. She kneeled beside him and petted his head.

"We got the results back from the lab," she said, looking at Oliver.

My stomach clenched. I hadn't expected to hear anything until Monday at the earliest. I wasn't ready to know. I thought I had four more days to pray.

"We got good news," she said, looking up and meeting my eye. I anticipated a "but" and held my breath. "The tumors were low Grade 2."

"At least it's not Grade 3," I said.

"There are only two grades now. Grade 1, low Grade 2, Grade 2, and high Grade 2."

"And which one did you say he has?"

"Low Grade 2."

"OK, OK." I wasn't sure what to think.

"The other thing we consider is the mitotic index. It gauges how fast the cancer cells are reproducing and measures on a scale from one to ten. Anything less than a five is promising, and a reading greater than five is a death sentence. Oliver scored very low—less than one."

She pulled out the report, and we went over it together. Based on studies, dogs with Oliver's levels had a survival rate of anywhere from two to seven years. One study showed an average of six years.

"That sounds pretty good."

Later, when I call Eden at school, she can hardly speak. I can tell she's on the verge of tears.

"From relief, Mama!" she will tell me when I pick her up later that afternoon.

Six years would put Oliver at the ripe old age of thirteen, and Eden into her senior year of high school.

"What's the next step?" I asked the doctor.

"I'm going to consult with the oncologist, and we'll decide what drug to use."

"What kind of time frame are we looking at?"

"Probably about four to six months of chemotherapy."

"My book manuscript is due to my editor in a month. I don't know what I'm going to say."

"You've still got your happy ending. Here's what you say: 'Oliver is responding well to chemotherapy and has every hope of living a long and happy life.'"

No promises, no guarantees, but every hope.

That's good enough for me.

Epilogue

Four months later

I'm working in the study today. Out the window above my desk, I can see across the street to where we stood on the path the morning of the fire and watched the house burn.

Today is the fifth anniversary.

I'm the only one home except for the dogs, asleep on one of their beds right in the doorway of the study. Oliver has been on chemo for four months and is doing well. Other than his fur looking a little browner in the sun, you would never know he was sick.

The bed he and Jack are sleeping on is normally in front of the bookcase next to my desk, but the floor is torn up and the room is a wreck. A month ago, I noticed water damage on the living room ceiling and the wall, and eventually we discovered the claw-foot tub had a leak and had soaked all three floors on the northwest corner of the house. It destroyed a built-in bookcase in the living room, as well as a section of the floor there and in the study, and part of the ceiling in the basement. (That tub!) It took weeks to get everything dried out, and a couple days later, we had a big party to celebrate Lydia's graduation. Life goes on, and through the chaos, we live, and even celebrate, around the mess. They start rebuilding next week.

Today is beautiful. There's a light breeze blowing through the trees and moving the clouds across the sky, so sometimes it's overcast and then the sun breaks through.

If I lean to the right, I can see the stop sign where the arsonist stopped his car that morning. I can't see the intersection because the three large white spruce trees we planted after the fire have grown and flourished and now shield the west side of our house from the street.

We still live at a crossroads—but then, all of us do. Aren't we all tempted to live with regrets from the past and worries about the future, when the invitation—the command, even—is to fully inhabit the glorious now of each day?

Soon Paul and Christopher will be home—and later, Eden. Lydia is house-sitting this week with Hope for another family friend—their first taste of independence. In a few hours, I'll quit work and go sit on the back porch while Paul grills dinner. I bought a couple old clamshell metal rocking chairs, and Paul and I like to sit there in the evening. We read and talk, and we listen to and watch the birds and admire the woods and gardens.

A nineteenth-century writer named Augustus Hare wrote, "To Adam Paradise was home. To the good among his descendants home is paradise."* My home in this world is Paul and the children, our extended family and friends, and—of course—the dogs. To be honest, it isn't always paradise, but it's a haven, which is so much more than enough.

---

*Augustus William Hare and Julius Charles Hare, *Guesses at Truth* (London: Macmillan, 1884), 243.

Acknowledgments

As I write these acknowledgments, I feel much like I felt after the fire—overwhelmed and undone by how many people have helped me, and unequal to the task of adequately and properly expressing my profound gratitude.

I'm thankful to Hope Harmon for allowing me to tell her piece of the story and for being the best and dearest friend to my girl.

Thanks to Ken and Claudie Vos, who, day after day and week after week, prayed me through some hard times during this writing.

I'm so grateful to my pastors—David Beelen, Joy Bonnema, and Darrell Delaney—and to the community of Madison Square Church for your wisdom, love, and prayerful support of our family for more than twenty years.

Thanks to Drs. Trish VanDenBrink and Kelly Juergensen and the entire staff at Ada Hospital for Animals, who have taken such good and compassionate care of all the Hodgsons—human and canine—through the years, and especially during Oliver's diagnosis and treatment.

Thanks to the indefatigably kind Sheila Schmitz, who gave me my start at Houzz.com, and to the Houzz community as a whole. The readers of Houzz are a haven of intelligence, civility, and fun in the Wild West that is the Internet.

The Pug List couldn't have found a better home than with Zondervan. I am unfailingly grateful to Stephanie Smith for first listening to my story and then for working so hard to help me tell it well. Thanks to David Morris and Alicia Kasen for welcoming me from the very beginning, and to Robin Barnett and Dirk Buursma for carrying me through to the end.

I owe profound thanks to the literary equivalent of a host of midwives, doulas, and loving aunties who helped me deliver:

Caryn Rivadeneira, Jennifer Grant, Michelle Van Loon, Marlena

Graves, Katherine Willis Pershey, Karen Swallow Prior, Andrea Dilley, Lesa Engelthaler, Helen Lee, Amy Julia Becker, Jen Pollock Michel, Gina Dalfonzo, Micha Boyett, Sharon Hodde Miller, Jessica Mesman Griffith, Gillian Marchenko, Halee Scott Gray, Tish Harrison Warren, Keri Wyatt Kent, and Laura Turner. Special thanks to Susy Flory and Dale Hanson Bourke for lending their expertise when I was writing the proposal, and to Ellen Painter Dollar for taking the time to cast her steely (and loving!) gaze over the manuscript.

To Rachel Marie Stone and "the Lisas"—Lisa Ann Cockrel and Lisa Beth Anderson—whose munificent hospitality opened a door, and to Kelly Hughes, who is simply the best.

To Jamie Chavez, kindred spirit and pal o' my heart, who has taught me so much and was bound and determined to help me find the right editor or agent, and did just that.

To the wonderful Mary Keeley, who took a chance on the idea of a book and expertly guided me through the publishing process.

So many thanks to Lorilee Craker for her incredible help and encouragement through the years, and to the rest of our beloved Guild: Tracy Groot, Ann Byle, Sharron Carrns, Shelly Beach, and Cynthia Beach for showing up the day after the fire with the "Oh Crap My House Burned Down!" survival kit: a pound of chocolate seafoam and a box of books—and even more importantly, for being there through the thick and thin of the years before and after the fire.

I don't know where I would be without family. Thanks to Thom and Dawn Longcore for picking us up by the side of the road. They were a haven for us long before the fire, and they continue to be still. Thanks to the rest of my Hodgson family for their love and for listening to my stories lo these many years. Barbara Hodgson, Greg and Sherree Hodgson, Jon and Kristi Marshall, and all my nieces and nephews—Andrew, Kristi, Megan, Ezra, Steven, Eli, Bethlehem, Simeon, Trevor, Eva, David, Grace, Sera, Sterling, and Jensen.

I'm forever grateful to my brothers Tanner Wolfe, Nathan Wolfe, and David Prinsen for being smart and funny and for helping me see things I otherwise wouldn't. To Torey Prinsen, my sister, first reader, and best friend—there isn't enough thanks for being who you are, and I couldn't love you more. Thanks to my nieces Ren and Willa Prinsen, who prayed for "Aunt Ali's book" every night, and to my mother, Marjorie Wolfe, who enrolled me in her grammar boot camp as soon as I began to speak. During this writing, she fed me a hundred lunches and prayed for me every day, and for years she has borne the burden of being proud enough for Dad too.

Most importantly, thank you to my own family, who so generously allowed me to tell our story. Christopher, Lydia, and Eden, I'm sorry almost any wisdom I have has been hard-won on your backs. I love you all so much. I'm glad I get to be your mom. Paul, the carpenters raised the roof beams higher in the new house, but they could never raise them high enough for a man so tall in every sense. I love you.

Thanks to Some Special Friends

We didn't know it at the time, but when we adopted Oliver, we also became members of Pug Nation. We are so grateful to have made friends all over the world, and when Oliver got sick, there was such an outpouring of love and support. I would like to thank just a few of our lovely friends on **Instagram** who helped Oliver make our days even more ridiculous and fun:

@157ofgemma @3pugpile @50shadesof.pug @alaskapuglife
@alfiethepug_beat @apugcalledpeggy @apugnamedemoji
@axltherunningpug @babycocoabean @banjopug
@bartho_the_pug @bodiepug @bostopug @brupert_bros
@bubblebeccapugs @buckleyclarkeadolf @buckthepugandfriends
@candy_pugs @canadianpugs @chloe_n_zoe @chickopugs
@chubbsthewampug @curlytailties @dailyomar
@dexidoo_dexterpug @dianegoldbach @dinaeastwood
@doobie_and_dawn @dq805 @dustythepug @ediethepug
@edthepug @elliedarciepugs @flossiethepug @fourfloridapugs
@frankie_jean_de_pug @frankiethepug_ @gilesthepug
@grumble_of_5 @grumpy_henry_the_pug @gwentheblackpug
@gusthecutepug @hamiltonpug @happypumbapug @hera_pug

@hercules_the_pug @homerpugalicious @ingo_mopsen
@insitu @its_a_pug_pug_world @itsluigithepug
@itsmaxthepug @kirbypug @kramboldt @lennon_and_jesse
@leoandgazgrl @leopoldthepug @lisagold18 @lord_gilroy
@lulu_and_coco @jakeythepug @justcallmepudge @maleffy
@maximusthecommander @meethercules @mevicchick
@milo_and_sophia_pug @minniemaxpugs @minnie_thepug
@mokatheadorablepug @mollyvecc @motoandmaggypugs
@nataliezmud @nickisparkles27 @odin_and_loki_of_asgard
@oliver_thepugpig @otisthepugwalsh @pauliepughamilton
@percypug27 @phinneausthepug @portiathepug @_posy
@pugalicious_vinny @pugbuddha_and_expo @pugdashians
@pugharleyandher3humans @pugridesshotgun @pugsngiggles
@pugporsche @realrufuspug @roccopugzworld @sammieseoul
@spankythepug @sprinkles_the_pug @simon_bella
@teddythepugx @thatsister_and_thechug @thebumblesnot
@thestylishbisou @thispugslife @tinyandbeastpugs @travisthepug
@thedutchpugsisters @twooldpugs @vaderpug @velvetpugears
@wasabithegreat

I would also like to thank our #PugChat friends on **Twitter** who, led by @hamiltonpug, make Wednesday nights the silly high point of our week:

@2blackpugz @AvaThePug47 @bambam_pug @carlypug
@chrischris716 @conchoqueen @EmmaThePug @funaek
@GrimNReaperPugs @knitonepugtwo @LeiniePug
@Maddrox_the_Pug @MissHannahPug @mollyg321 @pugjake
@pugmama4life @Sasha_Pug @snuggle_pugs @Spotneedsstuff
@StacyHRamirez @WoofWellington